FOR THE LOVE OF TEACHING

A PLEA FOR TRUST AND ENGAGEMENT

Mike Middleton

First published by Busybird Publishing 2021

Copyright © 2021 Michael Middleton

ISBN
978-1-922691-16-3 (paperback)
978-1-922691-17-0 (ebook)

This work is copyright. Apart from any use permitted under the *Copyright Act 1968*, no part of this publication may be reproduced, stored in a retrieval system or transmitted in any form or by any means, electronic, mechanical, photocopying, recording or otherwise, without the prior written permission of Michael Middleton.

The information in this book is based on the author's experiences and opinions. The author and publisher disclaim responsibility for any adverse consequences, which may result from use of the information contained herein. Permission to use any external content has been sought by the author. Any breaches will be rectified in further editions of the book.

Cover design: Busybird Publishing

Layout and typesetting: Busybird Publishing

Images: Michael Middleton

Busybird Publishing
2/118 Para Road
Montmorency, Victoria
Australia 3094
www.busybird.com.au

Dedicated to all those teachers yearning to be true to their calling as creative and innovative professional people, unafraid to think outside the box

Contents

Foreword	1
Introduction	3
Preface	5

PART 1 — 7

- Chapter 1 - My Schooling — 9
- Chapter 2 - Change of Career — 13
- Chapter 3 - Getting Serious — 19
- Chapter 4 - Tagari — 31
- Chapter 5 - Leaving Tasmania — 39
- Chapter 6 - Queensland and South Australia — 47
- Chapter 7 - A Tertiary Role — 61
- Chapter 8 - Self-Employment Adventures — 67
- Chapter 9 - Education at the Crossroads — 73
- Chapter 10 - A Melting Pot — 79
- Chapter 11 - Continuous Learning — 83
- Chapter 12 - New Basics or Subjects? — 91

PART 2 — 95

- Chapter 13 - Politics Intervenes — 97
- Chapter 14 - Effects of a Central Curriculum — 101

PART 3 — 109

- Chapter 15 - The Gonski Reports — 111
- Chapter 16 - Kids Are Different — 117
- Chapter 17 - Uncluttering The Curriculum — 125
- Chapter 18 - Buffered Spaces — 129
- Chapter 19 - POSTSCRIPT: Breaking the Lock-Step — 137

Conclusion	143
Bibliography	147
Acknowledgements	151

Foreword

I have a folder on my computer labelled 'Texts of Significance'. When I was asked by Michael (Mike) Middleton: "can you have a look at this draft and offer some ideas," I felt immensely privileged. My association with Mike goes back to his time as Chair of the Ministerial Council on Curriculum in Queensland and his longstanding and influential presence as an educational consultant. Having read the draft and now seen the finished work, both have been consigned to that special folder.

For the Love of Teaching is a deep reflection on educational practice by a practice focused exemplary educator. Its sub-title *A Plea for Trust and Engagement* highlights the personal investment by one of Australia's foremost thinkers and writers on what we now so commonly refer to as Praxis; the bringing together of quality research with quality teaching. The plea invites the reader into relationships with education that are founded in engagement, trust in oneself to exercise a disciplinary based reflection, and a not-so-subtle plea for integration and action.

Mike Middleton has achieved the almost impossible: being engaged in the process of education at the same time as being capable of its critique in context. His own leadership in education is immense, but more so is his ability to communicate the philosophy of education across boundaries and innovations that can lose sight of a past that informs, a present that demands, and a future that is hoped for. The text is a reminder to glance again at what has been evolving, being fascinated with the present moment, and in the process, consistently returning to the essence of what is valued most.

The experience of the author within multiple intersectoral educational settings across six decades provides more than a 'snapshot' of experiences, issues and emphases. We so often allude to the agency and witness of the teacher as the fundamental curriculum; and by implication, the assumption of integration of what is believed, expected and what works.

Mike's capture of his own experience and the expression of educational priorities and reflections is a must read as an exemplar of how to progress personally and professionally in a discipline that certainly challenges but importantly has the power to liberate.

For the love of Teaching is a refreshing and accessible reminder of the context of Australian education today and the importance of what historically and contemporaneously underpins national, provincial and local school aspirations. It stands alone in its unique presentation and will be a wonderful resource for students, leaders and policy makers who continue to ask questions about what has and continues to matter. It is without hesitation that the work is warmly and appreciatively received and endorsed as relevant for all educators. It has 'landed' in an important space, in a timely way, and in a fashion that impels 'the love of teaching'.

Dr William Sultmann AM
Australian Catholic University

Introduction

I started teaching sixty years ago. My daughter started three years ago. The contrast in her role as beginning teacher compared with mine in the 1960s could not be more extreme in terms of autonomy, professionalism and job satisfaction.

Having worked in Australian education for six decades, I have seen teaching decline from one of the preferred careers for graduates to one where universities have difficulty attracting able people into their teacher education courses. A significant percentage of new teaching graduates leave the profession in the first five years. I find this disappointing and distressing because my early experiences as a teacher were exciting, challenging and fulfilling – a career I would have recommended to anyone.

I began writing this three-part book in 2019, before the Covid-19 global pandemic. While the pandemic has had serious repercussions for some aspects of Australian education, particularly in the tertiary field, it may also productively have shaken loose some of the rigidity that has plagued Australian school education over the last two decades.

In this book, there are places where diagrams and illustrations are used to complement the text. This practice is reflective of my teaching habits in both the classroom and as a television presenter.

I hope readers of my generation will identify with the trends outlined in the three parts of this book and perhaps understand them better.

I hope policy makers at all levels will see possible ways ahead.

Most of all, I hope aspiring teachers will find inspiration that they too, given the chance, might enjoy teaching as much as I have.

Preface

I have chosen to write this book in three parts.

Part 1 traces the way formal education policy enhanced my life and the lives of my colleagues as educators until about 2005.

This part demonstrates what teaching was like for me and many of my fellow educators in the last five decades of the 1900s. As young teachers, we felt valued. Our opinions were important and we were encouraged to explore ideas and possibilities. Indeed, four of my close teaching friends and I were among many given paid time to travel overseas on scholarships to bring ideas back to share in our schools. As a young teacher, I had two Federal Education Ministers, John Gorton and Malcolm Fraser, later to become Prime Ministers, visit my classroom and talk with me about possibilities.

The chapters include snapshots of my sixty years of educational experience in turn as a student, teacher, curriculum developer, principal, ministerial adviser, lecturer and consultant. During the first fifty of these years, state and federal government policies were very supportive of teaching as a creative and innovative profession. I felt this strongly and put my heart and soul into my work. The fruitful interaction between policy and practice stimulated me and my colleagues to be the best we could be. Hopefully, the journey shared might encourage young and aspiring teachers to see that, with the appropriate support, teaching can be a creative, exciting and fulfilling career.

Part 2 describes the sudden political changes that severely affected not only my life as an educator, but also the lives of many in my profession.

Changes in government policy impinged on my career, and on teachers' work generally. The changes were inherently political in nature and still threaten to reduce teachers from members of a creative and noble profession to functionaries, staffing yearly delivery stations on an educational assembly line.

Part 3 addresses the recent Gonski and NSW Reviews and suggests ways in which their important recommendations might be implemented.

These reviews acknowledge the failures of the recent decades and make broad recommendations to redirect education policy. However, these and other reports will fail to bear fruit unless ways are found of reversing a change model that is essentially 'top-down' to one that is 'bottom-up', as change was in the latter half of the 1900s. Two kinds of initiatives are suggested. A way in which the necessary shift to a 'bottom up' dynamic might be achieved is suggested. Some grass roots initiatives are then described as catalysts for a more creative and adaptive professional life for teachers and a better set of outcomes for students.

I am aware that there are wonderful teachers currently working in Australian schools. I acknowledge their enthusiasm, skill and passion. In no way do I intend this book to devalue their work. My hope is that many more such wonderful teachers will enter the profession over the coming decades.

PART 1

Chapter 1
My Schooling

I started my schooling in the immediate post-war years. Because my father was an ex-serviceman looking for a job, I went to seven different primary schools in Victoria and Tasmania. My final primary year was at Trevallyn State School in Launceston. In those days, Tasmanian students did an 'ability test' to determine which of three kinds of secondary school they would attend. Those with the highest marks went to high school. Those who just missed out went to technical school. The others went to secondary modern school.

Trevor Rushton, who was in my grade six class, went to Brooks secondary modern school. He tells me he failed deliberately because he wanted to go to Brooks to learn farming. He later spent 23 years as managing director of a flooring company. My older brother Ren went to Launceston Technical School. I have been jealous of him all my life because he got to use hammers and saws and lathes. He built things, including boats.

I was sent to Launceston High School. I had no choice but to 'do' French and German which I have never used. I tell a lie. When I was in year 10, my mate and I were caught in a storm on our family launch. We tried, illegally, to moor at the pilot station near the mouth of the Tamar River at Low Head. Two officials ran down to the jetty to tell us we couldn't moor there. I shouted to them my recently learned German oral. *"Achtung, bissiger hund, und richtig. Hinter der tur des hauses lag ein hund and wolte niemand hineinlassen."*

"The buggers don't speak English," one said to the other.

"We'd better let them stay," said the other, shrugging his shoulders.

As we began high school in 1952, none of the kids was dropped off by parents in cars as many are today. Apart from those who lived out of town and came in by school bus, everyone either walked or rode their bikes. Indeed, the largest building on the Launceston High School grounds was the bike shed. A man called Lofty ruled the bike shed. He was actually the groundsman, but his relationship with the boys was closer than that of many of the teachers. For example, as the Suez crisis blew up during the mid-1950s, it was Lofty we went to when we really wanted to know what was going on.

Our high school teachers were very different from each other in their personalities, their teaching styles and their beliefs. It was their uniqueness as people that I remember most. Max Poulter taught Social Science. He had very strong left wing political views and later became a Labor senator in Queensland. 'Deutchy' Damien was our German teacher. He didn't teach us much German, but he taught us a lot about being human. He was a pilot during World War II, was shot down over North Africa and captured by Australian soldiers. Their treatment of him inspired him to migrate to Australia after the war. Loris Russell, my English teacher, motivated me to love writing. Bill Phillips was our cricket coach. He also taught geology. I chose to study geology at matriculation level because I liked Bill. My happy memories of high school are much more about socialising and sport than they are about the formal learning I experienced.

I left school in 1957.

Over the next three years, while I was at university, selective secondary education in Tasmania disappeared. The ability test separating children into three kinds of schools was suddenly abandoned and Tasmanian state secondary school students attended 'comprehensive' schools that catered for all categories of student under the one roof. By 1959, there were many of these new comprehensive schools in the planning stages. They were planned with facilities not just for academic learning, but for technical studies and home economics.

As explained later, the change in Tasmania was extremely rapid and not fully thought through. This resulted in two major difficulties. The first involved what to do with the selective high schools in Hobart, Launceston, Devonport and Burnie that had inadequate facilities for technical subjects or home economics. The second difficulty involved an extreme shortage in the number of specialist academic teachers needed to teach years 11 and 12 in all of the planned 'comprehensive' schools. The hasty solution was to convert the previous selective high schools into centralised 'matriculation colleges' solely for years 11 and 12. The comprehensive schools catered only for years 7 to 10.

Other Australian states took decades to do what Tasmania did in a few years. These states also moved towards a comprehensive pattern but without the need for senior colleges. Students stayed in the same school throughout their secondary years.

Debates about the pros and cons of selective secondary schooling occurred in all states. Most maintained, and still have, some selective government secondary schools. Victoria's last junior technical schools were discontinued in the 1980s as a result of the Blackburn Report (1985) which recommended a comprehensive system.[1] However, it is interesting to note that, during the 2014 election campaign, opposition Labor leader, Daniel Andrews, promised "to bring back technical schools". Andrews claimed that "Victorian students deserve a head start on a hands-on profession."[2] He argued the loss of the history of former technical schools could perpetuate mistakes made in the past and be less than useful in helping students take their place in society. There were strong reasons for recalling their characteristics to modern educators, he believed.

NSW made a decision in 1967 (Wyndham Report) to replace its selective system with a comprehensive pattern.[3] However, there had been a long history of selective government schooling in that state and many of the graduates of the top selective high schools were influential in defending these schools. In 2019, 48 secondary schools in NSW that were fully or partially selective remained.

During the 1960s and 1970s, South Australia, Western Australia and Queensland all moved to patterns that were dominantly comprehensive although in 2020, these states still had some schools that were selective, either from year 7 or year 9. Many of the early comprehensive schools in Australia provided different courses for students, depending on their abilities and aspirations. In this sense, they were really multilateral, with an internal tripartite system where students were 'streamed' into different courses.

Chapter 2
Change of Career

University life in Tasmania was a stark contrast to my high school experience. It was a grind. I had to work hard to achieve. There was little time for sport or socialising. Because I studied science, and in particular geology and geophysics, the student numbers were small and, for the most part, exclusively male. I had no female friends while I was at university.

When I finished my three years studying for a science degree, I took a job as geophysicist with the Bureau of Mineral Resources.

This involved undertaking a geo-magnetic survey of the iron ore deposits in the Savage River area of the Tarkine wilderness in northwestern Tasmania. I worked with a geology graduate. Our first job, before we could undertake a magnetic survey, was to cut a straight track ten miles to the south of our open campsite, as precursor to a rectangular grid of tracks.

> TRA-91-92
> **PROPOSED GEOPHYSICAL INVESTIGATIONS BY THE BUREAU OF MINERAL RESOURCES FOR 1960**
> by T. D. Hughes.
>
> Following a visit with Dr. Horvath of the Bureau to the areas concerned, we have suggested the following programme:—
> **I. SAVAGE RIVER IRON ORE DEPOSITS**
> 1. Survey of lines already cut and pegged to the south of the area already investigated, that is south of "A" line. There will be six traverses, 500 feet apart and averaging 1500 feet in length.
>
> Geologist P. Tetlow has been instructed to prepare the following work for a Bureau Geophysicist, who should be ready to carry out a magnetometer survey late in January.

We soon discovered that this wasn't going to be easy. The rainforest was thick, too thick to see the sky or the sun. The hills were very steep. To complicate matters, the magnetic iron ore virtually froze a compass needle making it useless. (I learned later that in 1642 Abel Tasman, sailing south along Tasmania's west coast, noted similar issues with the ship's compass and wrote in his log an entry that translated "there must be mines of lodestone about here").

We could establish 'south' at the open campsite by the direction of shadows at noon. We decided to cut two sticks and jam them into the ground, one due south of the other. Then as we cut the track southwards, we could keep using sticks, making sure they were always in a straight line behind us. Problem solved. We congratulated ourselves.

After about two weeks with axes and slashers and a measuring tape, we figured we'd got about halfway. Despite it being hard work, we enjoyed the challenge. The rainforest was beautiful. Small creeks were adorned with overhanging waratahs. It was truly an untouched 'Garden of Eden'. Our only contact with the outside world was a transistor radio I carried so that we could listen to the Test Cricket between Australia and the West Indies. The first test in Brisbane was drawn – I remember hearing it while we were sitting beside a stream.

About this time, two four-wheel drives appeared at the campsite delivering six Tasmanian bush-cutters from the town of Waratah about thirty miles away to the east. Apparently, the powers that be were getting impatient. The bushmen's task was to cut a similar ten-mile track to the north of the campsite. These were rugged individuals, very fit and skilled with axes and slashers. Their spoken language was fairly florid, typical of their time and culture. We shared evenings with them around the fire and enjoyed their stories and their company. They went about their work and finished their track about the same time as we finished ours.

The next visitors were two surveyors who mapped the tracks that had been cut. To my astonishment, they intimated that the track south was about thirty degrees out over the ten miles while the track to the north was only six degrees out. This did nothing for my ego. After all, I had completed a major in geophysics, and these were 'illiterate' bushmen. George was the most vocal and cocky of them. One evening, while chatting with George, I asked

"By the way George, how did you guys get your track straight?"

"Well, we f... ing thought about that. Then we decided to use my transistor. We turned it around till it was loudest and then scratched a bloody great north arrow on the leather case. It seemed to work."

Lesson number one!

Exciting and often amusing though it was, the Savage River experience also had its drawbacks. It was isolating for a twenty-year-old to spend months without seeing a house or a car or a telephone or a girl! The pride I felt in helping map the deposit magnetically was deflated when I realised that our find would result in the total destruction of many square miles of beautiful rainforest. Adding to my disenchantment, the contract to ship the iron ore sludge to Japan for processing was won by an American shipping company. Was my work doing anything really good for Tasmania – or the world?

On a day off in Waratah, I telephoned the Tasmanian Education Department to enquire about teaching.

"Do you have teacher training?"

"No."

"Well what do you have?"

"I have majors in geology and geophysics."

There was a pause and a shuffling of papers.

"There's a position for a science teacher at R.M. Murray High School in Queenstown. Could you start next week?"

I was taken aback and didn't answer straight away.

"Well?"

"Yeah sure," I said, "Where will I live?"

"There's a teachers' hostel, so that won't be a problem."

So began the rest of my life.

In 1961, Queenstown miners were mining the copper ore of Mount Lyell. Others were smelting and refining the copper. The school students were mainly the sons and daughters of miners and mine workers. At the first morning assembly, I gained an impression of them. Many seemed to have the same kind of outlook on life as the bushmen I had met on the Savage

River some miles to the north. I felt OK about that. My first class was a low stream year 9 class, mostly boys. I was told that the next thing they needed to learn about was the human alimentary canal and digestive system.

"There's a set of textbooks you can use. *Biology for Australian Students* by Winifred Curtis."

I had a look at the book, flipped through the appropriate section and decided that some of the kids would probably have difficulty reading it and wouldn't be excited even if they did.

I took a couple of apples and a vegetable knife into the class. After introducing myself and getting a few g'days from kids trying to sus me out, I held up the two apples.

"Do you reckon you kids could eat these apples hanging upside down on the parallel bars out there in the playground?"

That started them off.

"Course you couldn't, the apple would fall into your head."

"You've got brains you idiot, how could it?"

There followed several minutes of general give and take and then I called a halt.

"It seems some of you think you could, and others think you couldn't. Hands up those who think you could …. OK, well you guys have a theory – scientists call it a hypothesis. We have two hypotheses – some think you can, and some think you can't. How do you reckon we could find out who is right?"

"Don't know."

"Scientists test their hypotheses. Let's go outside."

Wide-eyed wonder.

There we were with some kids hanging upside down on the bars while others lay on the sloping grassy bank, trying to eat pieces of apple.

The deputy principal came out and said that I should try to get some teacher education.

When we got back to the classroom, the kids were full of questions.

"How does that happen then? I thought the food sort of fell into our stomach."

I used the example of a toothpaste tube to explain how the muscles work. I talked about the oesophagus and how the muscular squeezing was called peristalsis.

"I never knew that."

And then as they left the room, I overheard.

"Well I'll be buggered!"

Thus ended my first lesson. I was hooked already. This was fun, finding ways to get kids to understand was an exciting challenge, even if my behaviour management needed some tweaking! Maybe if I make things really interesting, it won't matter.

Chapter 3
Getting Serious

In 1962, aged 22, I was transferred to the new Clarence High School on Hobart's eastern shore. It was a comprehensive school of over a thousand students, called a high school to give it status. The school was a young teacher's heaven. The headmaster, Eddy Smith, was a wonderful educator. He encouraged us to think creatively. He tended to say 'yes' to well planned projects. I taught science and maths. In the 1960s, science was not a formal part of the primary school curriculum so that many students looked forward to learning science in the laboratories of secondary schools. I loved the challenge of teaching chemistry and physics so that students would understand and internalise the concepts and love the learning. It was a matter of making the discipline live. When I had a new chemistry class in year 9, I would tell them to close their eyes and relax. Then quietly I would say.

"How sweet the moonlight sleeps upon this bank."

Long pause.

"Open your eyes."

"Hands up who saw grass?"

"Who saw trees?"

"Who saw water?"

"Who saw clouds?"

With a table prepared on the blackboard, it would only take four or five questions to demonstrate that no two students in a class of twenty-four imagined the same kind of scene.

"That's the genius of Shakespeare. He was able to stimulate a range of images from a simple text. In science, we try to do the opposite. Can we report so that all readers will make exactly the same interpretation? We need to try."

Linking science to other disciplines provided students with a rich context. I demonstrated the reactions of various metals by placing small samples in a trough of water or dilute acid. Potassium and sodium really fizzed, exciting the students. Calcium bubbled, as did zinc and iron in dilute acid. But copper and silver had no reaction. I explained that human history was closely linked to the reactivity of metals. Some, like gold and silver, could be found untainted because they did not react with water or air or other solutions found on Earth. They were the 'noble metals', first to be found. However, most metals had to be 'extracted' from their ores. In this way, I was able to link human history with the reactivity of metals starting with the stone age, before metals were discovered, through the bronze and iron ages to the industrial revolution and to humanity's later ability to extract by electrolysis more reactive metals like lithium, calcium, sodium, potassium and aluminium that didn't occur on their own in nature.

So that students would be able to understand formulae and manipulate chemical equations, I developed my own simplified way of representing atoms, molecules and radicals. Metals had one or more 'beaks'. Non-metals had one or more 'notches'. Beaks fitted into notches.

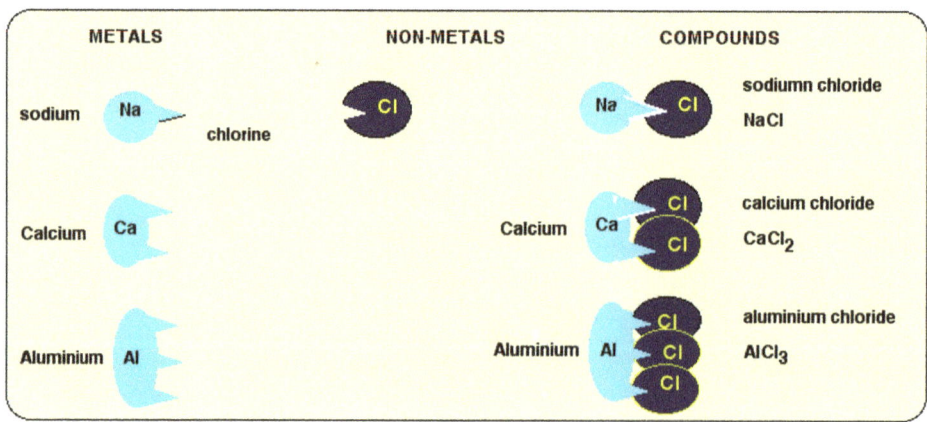

Inert gases had neither beaks nor notches. They could not combine with anything.

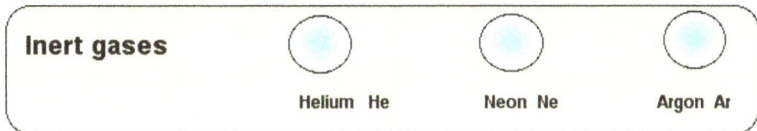

Carbon was really special. It could behave as either a metal with 'beaks' or a non-metal with 'notches'. It could therefore combine in countless ways to create really complex molecules. This made the evolution of life possible.

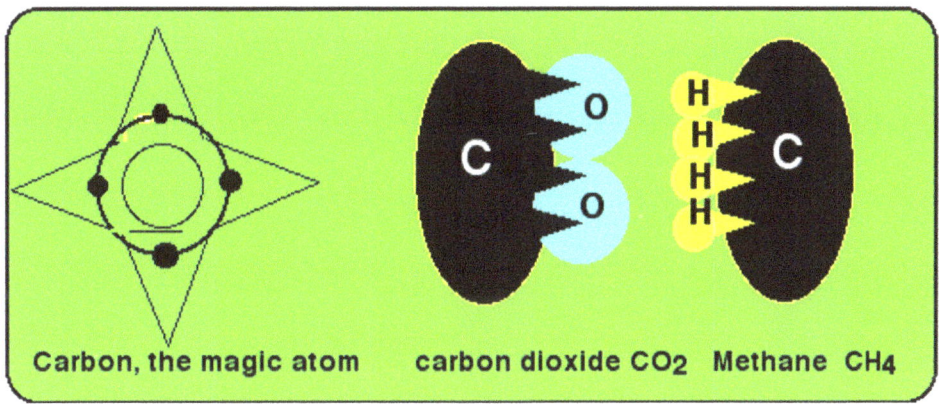

Because of this versatility, carbon is the common factor in all living things. I did not need, at this early stage, to explain the shell structures of atoms. I wanted to make the learning exciting. Once the kids were hooked, almost all wanted to learn about the complexities.

It was like an early 'Lego'. The kids loved the patterns and used them effectively to write the chemical equations for the reactive experiments they undertook in the laboratory. The point I am making here is that I developed my own approach to teaching. It was customised and designed for my own students. It couldn't and shouldn't be mindlessly duplicated. It worked for me and my students. Other teachers would find their own ways, sharing each other's ideas. This was part of the culture of teaching in those days.

John Holt, who was writing at the time, greatly influenced my teaching. He was an American educator who began his teaching career after a stint in the Navy. He wrote a number of books about teaching and learning during the 1960s and 1970s. I identify with him because, like me, he entered the teaching profession without any training. It may be that this lack of formal induction allowed him to see the teaching role more objectively and more freshly than most. One book by John Holt had a very strong impact on me. It was titled *What do I do Monday?*[4]

In this book Holt considered the kinds of learning that students undertake. Using a metaphor that he titled the "worlds I live in", he described four such worlds.

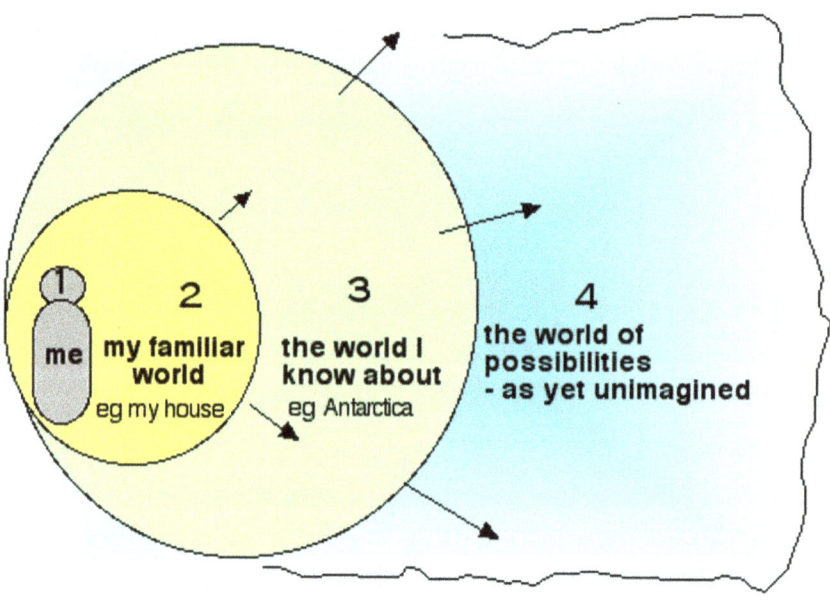

World 1 is the world inside my skin. I nurture it and it grows.

World 2 is the world I am familiar with. It is uniquely mine. My bedroom, my parents, my neighbourhood. It grows as I experience the world directly through my senses.

World 3 is the world I know about. I learn about this world from books, from films and from the words and descriptions of other people.

World 4 is the boundless world of possibilities I haven't yet heard about or imagined.

I never thought of my teaching as 'delivering' a curriculum to my students. It was much more about creating circumstances, images, ideas and challenges that stimulated them to engage in an exciting learning journey, expanding their worlds 2 and 3. I liked involving my students in my teaching. For example, I developed an acronym for the kids in my first chemistry class to remember the order in which metals reacted. It's called the electro-chemical series. There was a girl in the class called Sue Head who was a real character, capable of laughing at herself and popular in the group.

My acronym read

'Poor Sue couldn't make a zac in her copper. Most silly girl.'

Poor	potassium	
Sue	sodium	
Couldn't	calcium	
Make	magnesium	
A	aluminium	HUMAN HISTORY
Zac	zinc	
In	iron	
Her	hydrogen	
Copper	copper	
Most	mercury	
Silly	silver	
Girl	gold	

That was nearly sixty years ago. I have lately spoken with some ex-students who were in that class. They still remember the acronym, the series and the historical links.

I found that the metaphor of dancing also helped students understand chemical reactions and balancing equations. Double decomposition was swapping partners. Decomposition was 'splitting up'. Displacement was 'tapping on the shoulder' to take over a partner. Inert gases just danced alone. Sometimes, we would undertake dances in the laboratory either to teach a reaction or for students to demonstrate their understanding of it. A number of them later became professionals in various fields of science.

Lots of kids found mathematics boring, difficult or both. I found the best way to engage them was to be very hands-on. For example, we ran week-long year 9 'maths camps' at Turners Beach in northern Tasmania. There were lots of opportunities. I would take a small group down to the eastern bank of the Forth River with a compass and a measuring tape. (No GPS in those days).

"I'll give you till lunch time to find out how wide the river is."

"But it's too wide and deep. We can't get across."

"I know."

"Well how can we do it?"

"Think about it."

Over a couple of hours and after much discussion and argument, kids invariably developed their own ways of measuring the width of the river and in the process discovered some of the secrets of geometry. Some students also began to appreciate that trigonometry wasn't just for textbooks.

"Is that how Matthew Flinders mapped the coastline without going ashore?"

"Same kind of thinking. How about measuring the height of that big eucalypt?"

After a couple of years of teaching, I was asked to join a small team to design and present the ABC's Science for Schools TV series. Challenged and stimulated, I presented about fifty black and white programs, each of twenty minutes, that were broadcast to secondary schools across the nation. I made about one program a fortnight, while I was teaching full time. The classroom teaching helped me try out ideas for the programs. It was demanding and challenging work. There were no computers then. We had to work closely with the graphics department to design visuals.

Some of the programs were outside broadcasts where we explored lighthouses, geological features and mines. One series of six programs was made on Tasmania's west coast, exploring the geology, the topography and the history of mining.

The Russians had launched Sputnik in 1957. Six years later, the Australian Federal Government decided it was time to become involved in the science curriculum. It boosted funding for libraries and laboratories in schools. John Gorton was Minister for Education and Science. He initiated the Australian Science Education Project (ASEP). A minimum of three states was required for the Project to go ahead with federal funding; Victoria, South Australia and Tasmania opted in. I was nominated as Tasmania's representative on the team to help foster it. The team met in Melbourne and I trialled the program in my own junior classes, being visited in my laboratory by John Gorton in the process. This was my first experience of a national initiative in Australian education, and it was a very positive one.

I taught at Clarence High School for nine years. Every day, I was excited about my work and about the students I was teaching. I hadn't done any initial teacher training but there was a shortage of science teachers in Australia and this provided me with great opportunities. In retrospect, I realise that at least 70% of my professional time was actually face-to-face teaching. This was because the students sat for external exams at the end of their course, leaving me free of the burden of constant formal assessments that encumber many teachers currently. I didn't need formal assessments to know whether individual students were excelling or struggling. The classroom dynamics were such that I was constantly aware of students who needed help with particular skills or concepts, or who needed extension. I felt like a coach.

In 1967, I was asked to make the school timetable for 1968. This changed my life. At first, I tried to follow the lead of the previous timetablers. But, as I worked, I began to ask myself questions about the organisation of schools in Australia generally. I analysed the process.

- ◊ Divide the curriculum into subjects.
- ◊ Divide the school into rooms.
- ◊ Divide the time into 'periods' of 35 minutes.
- ◊ Divide the teaching staff into individuals.
- ◊ Divide the students into year groups and then into classes within the year groups.

The job was to make sure that during any given period, each class within the year group was matched with a subject, a room, and a teacher. As long as there was no class left unmatched, and no teacher overloaded, the timetable 'worked'.

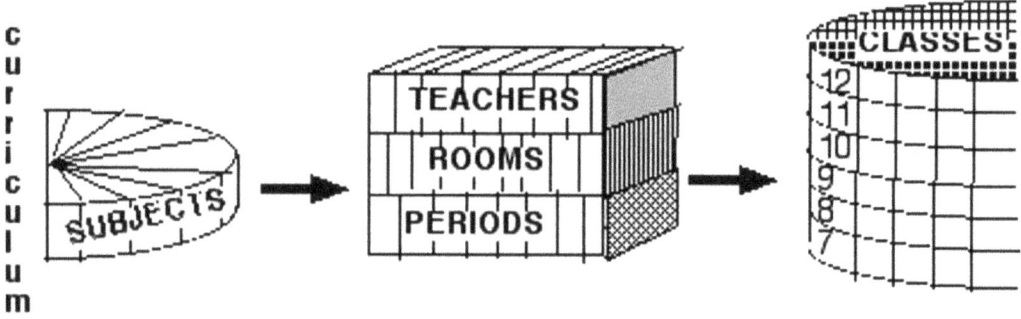

I had two main problems with the process. First, it was so complex that only the timetabler really understood it. For teachers and for students, this was disempowering. The timetablers were gatekeepers who could say 'yes' or 'no' to suggestions (often depending on how much extra work it would mean for them). Innovation was in danger of being stifled because people didn't know what was possible.

Second, it didn't seem to make sense to have students grouped strictly according to age. For me, an ex-geophysicist, it seemed medieval that every time the Earth completed an orbit around the Sun, all students moved on a step, irrespective of what they had learnt previously, or in what part of the orbit they were born. (How long would an academic year be if we ever settled on Mars?) It was obvious to me that people learn at different rates. I found some students bored because they already knew what was being 'taught'. Others were being forced ahead before they were ready. (Sometimes, those who take more time to master something end up experts like Einstein, who didn't talk until he was three.) I began to think of alternative patterns of organisation.

During the late 1960s, schooling initiatives in the United Kingdom included the newly created comprehensive schools in London and the middle schools in the West Riding. My interest in these developments led me to apply successfully to the Tasmanian Education Department for a year-long 1971 travelling scholarship, based in London. It is significant that, during the 1960s, the Tasmanian government was keen to send young teachers overseas. This was not, in any way, a reward for their work. It was a means of bringing ideas into the state to feed debates and encourage innovation. How different things are now. In those days, airfares were so expensive that it was better to go by ship. We sailed on the liner Iberia from Melbourne, through Fremantle, Durban, Cape Town, Senegal, Las Palmas and Lisbon to Southampton.

On arrival, it didn't take me long to realise that living in England was not like living in Hobart. The unit we rented in Beckenham, Kent, was adjacent to the railway station. On the first morning, I set out to catch a train to London's Victoria Station. I joined a score of commuters on the platform and waited for the train. In due course, a train labelled 'Victoria' came to a stop at the station. I walked forward to open the carriage door. Suddenly, the stationmaster blew his whistle and ran towards me.

"You can't get on that train!" he yelled.

"Why not?" I asked.

"It doesn't stop here."

I raised my eyebrows and pointed to the train.

"It's only stopped for the signal," he said.

In London, it pays to be in the know.

When I finally made it to Victoria Station and the nearby office of the UK Inspectorate, I quickly learned that English educators were struggling with the same dilemmas I was. There was much discussion about the pros and cons of 'streaming'. This was a major issue because, for many, streaming within schools was seen to be little better than the streaming between schools that had occurred previously. Arguments against streaming asserted that the practice would separate children based on their socio-economic background or their racial background. In any case, a good teacher ought to be able to cater for a wide range of students in the one class. Others argued that, without streaming, talented students would be held back, struggling students would lose interest and teachers would find it difficult to cope. Nobody talked about what I saw as the elephant in the room – the fact that the age grading of students actually created the problem. You couldn't be accelerated so you had to be 'streamed'. I was asked to address a London principals' conference about my dilemmas and my approach to timetabling.

The fact that it was cheaper in 1971 to travel to and from England by ship than it was by plane meant about ten weeks at sea because the Suez Canal was closed. Ten weeks provided plenty of time for reading, and I was stimulated by the educational thinking that was occurring. In particular, I remember reading books by John Dewey, Neil Postman, Ivan Illich and Paulo Freire. A quote from each of these thinkers encapsulates the attitudes towards education that were being debated.

I had read Dewey earlier. This quote from the preface of his book *Experience and Education* (1938) had a real impact on my thinking.

"Education is not preparation for life; education is life itself."[5]

In *Teaching as a Subversive Activity*, (1971) Neil Postman and Charles Weingartner wrote:

"There is no way to help a learner to be disciplined, active, and thoroughly engaged unless he perceives a problem to be a problem or whatever is to-be-learned as worth learning, and unless he plays an active role in determining the process of solution."[6]

Ivan Illich was perhaps the best known of the writers because he talked about 'deschooling society'. He didn't want to get rid of schools. He wanted them to be more than institutions that conditioned young people to accept their world without question.

"Most learning is not the result of instruction. It is rather the result of unhampered participation in a meaningful setting. Most people learn best by being 'with it' yet school makes them identify their personal, cognitive growth with elaborate planning and manipulation."[7] (*Deschooling Society*, 1971).

Paulo Freire was a Brazilian Catholic priest. He wrote *Pedagogy of the Oppressed*,[8] a book that was translated into English from Portuguese in 1970. The Australian Student Christian Movement invited him to Australia in the early 1970s. I later had the pleasure and honour of spending some days with him at a conference in Mt Eliza, Victoria. Two of his concepts had particular meaning for me. The first was what he called 'the banking concept'. He believed that too often the process of schooling was like making deposits in a bank. The teacher did the depositing and the students were the passive, uncritical receptors of what was delivered to them. The second concept was that of 'conscientisation'. This stressed how important it was for people to understand the context in which they were getting messages or having activities organised for them. Only so could they avoid being 'domesticated', as Freire put it, or being 'schooled', as Illich termed it.

Shortly after I returned from England, Gough Whitlam was elected Prime Minister of Australia, a position he held from 1972 to 1975. These three years saw changes in Australian education, the ramifications of which are still felt today. For me, an enthusiastic and deeply committed teacher, he was inspirational. He established the Australian Schools Commission and initiated a review of Australian schooling. This review was carried out by a committee chaired by Professor Peter Karmel [9]. Its report stressed that the Commonwealth should not become involved in the administration of schools and school systems in the states. Rather, it should determine priorities and the provision of resources. Authority should be decentralised to the local school community and schools should provide diversity in structure, curricula and teaching methods. The committee stressed the need for education to be as equal as possible for all students, enabling them to reach standards necessary for life in a modern democratic industrial society. This was music to my ears; it encouraged me and my colleagues to continue exploring new approaches to our work.

I was asked to join the Hobart-based committee responsible for distributing the Karmel funds in Tasmania. On first reading, there appeared to be a contradiction built into the recommendations. How could education be equal when the report also recommended a high degree of diversity in structures, curricula and pedagogy? It took some discussion for us to appreciate what the committee members were espousing. They knew that students were inevitably situated in a wide variety of social, economic, cultural and geographic circumstances. If they were all to achieve an education that would prepare them for participation in a future Australia, their pathways to achievement would necessarily be very different. Local communities and teaching teams were the most capable of making the necessary judgements about what was best for their particular students – providing the resources were available and providing there were clear guidelines and professional support. The Committee recommended a number of categories of Commonwealth expenditure. These included funding for buildings and libraries as well as needs-based recurrent expenditure. There was also a focus on special education and disadvantaged schools.

If our Tasmanian committee was to be true to the Karmel recommendations, we had to take seriously the ability of the whole system to adapt to change, and in some areas, to lead change. This could not occur in a monolithic system. It would only occur if there was a range of initiatives being undertaken by schools and systems, with good communication between them. Individual school experiences provided important indications about the likely outcomes of particular initiatives. A biological analogy that I remember hearing at the time related to Darwinian thinking. An animal or plant species only adapts successfully to a changing environment if there is a wide variety of characteristics among its members and these members are in fertile interaction with each other. We realised it should be so with schools. Of particular interest to me was 'The Innovations Program'. It was designed to stimulate diversity by encouraging and funding well planned initiatives.

Chapter 4

Tagari

A year in England and wide reading had given me a chance to reflect on the structures of schooling. Though they wouldn't necessarily have expressed it this way, many people, including educators, saw schools like assembly line factories. Little kids came in. Each year, new learnings were 'added' to them, and after ten or eleven years of processing, they came out as big kids, measured to enter an appropriate level in society and become part of the economy as producers and consumers. The school was a permanent bureaucracy and a permanent physical processing structure. The humans, even teachers, were just temporary tenants passing through. The Whitlam Innovations Project provided me with the potential to test whether this was the only, or even the best, way of thinking about school education. I envisaged an alternative pattern where students didn't 'go to' school, rather, students *were* the school – a community of learners.

I wrote a proposal that would involve fifty year 6 students leaving primary school in 1973. Instead of going to one of the existing high schools for years 7 to 10, they would undertake their learning in the natural and social environment, utilising a base in the city of Hobart, but spending a percentage of their time away from Hobart, either camping or in other accommodation. I invited a recommended humanities teacher from Rose Bay High School, Fran Bladel, to join me as co-teacher. Athol Gough, the Director-General of Tasmanian Education, negotiated with the Commonwealth Schools Commission. If the application was successful, we were to remain employees of the Tasmanian Education Department and the Project would be administered through the Research Branch of that department. We were very happy with this arrangement. We sent the proposal to the Innovations Section of the newly formed Schools Commission. Several weeks later, I received a visit from Joan Kirner and Jean Blackburn who discussed the project with me and gave it the go-head, provided there were at least forty families prepared to participate.

Anxiously, we prepared a flyer and sent it to the parents of year 6 students in the state primary schools around Hobart. The information provided was very simple. The Project was to open in 1974. It would be based in rented premises in Hobart. There would be no uniform. Parental involvement would be paramount. The curriculum would include outdoor activities, a wide range of electives and would make use of the resources of the city and beyond. Within a week, there were about six hundred applications. Fifty-two students were chosen at random by the Research Branch. They represented a socio-economic cross section of Hobart families that had enrolled their sons and daughters in state primary schools.

The funding for the project provided the possibility of three full-time teachers. Between us, Fran and I had the experience and skill to teach most of the mainstream subjects like maths, science, English, History and Geography. We chose to use the funding for a third teacher flexibly, utilising about forty hours per week of part-time teaching. Our first base was a hall attached to the Wesley Church. After a few weeks, we relocated briefly to the YMCA and finally to a vacant house in Battery Point that the students had discovered. The students chose to call themselves Tagari, an Aboriginal word meaning family.

The greatest mental challenge for me was to 'let go', so that the kids were able to make significant decisions about what they would learn and how they would learn it. For example, we asked them what foreign languages they would like to learn. The variety of their choices was challenging – Latin, German, Italian, Spanish and French. Our flexibility in terms of part-time teaching allowed us to offer all of these.

One of the interesting programs some of the students invented was called 'people and people'. It took place on Wednesday afternoons while we were in Hobart. They had a list of people they wanted to talk with, including Aboriginal leader Michael Mansell, communist leader Derek

Roebuck, nuns, university students, painters and politicians. They would research the person and their role one Wednesday afternoon and then interview them the following Wednesday. I learnt as much as the kids did.

The group, along with some of the parents, spent about a hundred days and nights away from Hobart, including most areas of Tasmania as well as Central Australia and parts of Victoria and South Australia. We also used Hobart's social and physical environment. Two memories stand out. We caught a local bus to the peak of nearby Mount Wellington and spent the day studying the plants as we walked back down. We studied in turn algae, fungi, lichens, mosses, liverworts, ferns, conifers and flowering plants. What better way of introducing them to the evolution of plants on Earth? I regretted that in the previous decade of teaching science in Hobart, I had relied on films, textbooks and samples to teach the same thing.

The other outstanding memory involves Stephen and Peter. I had asked students to choose an aspect of the local Battery Point environment to study in depth. Some chose the history, some tourism, some the restaurants and some the architecture. Stephen and Peter chose the traffic. A couple of weeks later, as the groups presented their reports, I had to question Stephen's and Peter's methodology because they had drawn graphs showing the traffic density over a week, 24 hours a day. I explained that it wasn't valid to extrapolate or to guess traffic flows when they weren't there to observe it.

"I think you'd better come with us," Stephen said.

They led the way and showed me two rubber tubes stretched across a road. I was taken aback.

"You'd best explain," I said.

They explained that they figured the Department of Transport would know most about traffic in Battery Point and that they would go there and ask about it. They were offered the chance to measure the traffic flow using the Department's apparatus, as long as they recorded it regularly and reported back to the Department. This kind of community involvement was bread and butter to the Tagari students as they grew in confidence. Other students later joined with police to build kayaks.

The Battery Point house had an old stable that we used as an art studio. For the first three years, Eloise had been the art teacher. However, she was unable to continue for the fourth year, so we had to find a new art teacher. I used the opportunity to teach the art students something about employment.

"I want you guys to choose the next art teacher."

"How do we do that?"

I explained that they should put an advertisement in the local paper. Then they could create a shortlist, interview the applicants and choose the person they felt would teach them best. That is what happened. Interestingly, several applicants were uneasy about being interviewed by students and withdrew. (I saw it as perfect self-selection). The teacher the students chose was not someone I would have chosen – but she was perfect for the job.

When 1977 finished and the group disbanded, Fran and I sought to repeat the process with a second group. However, the embarrassing memory of the application pressure four years earlier discouraged the Minister and departmental people from repeating the exercise.

In 1978, the Tasmanian Government commissioned Professor William Connell to write a report recommending developments in Tasmanian education over the next decade. This was called the TEND Report. It commented as follows on Tagari:

"…even very small schools, such as the 50 student experimental school, Tagari, have been able to provide a richer variety (of courses) than many large schools by judicious use of community resources and part-time staff. There seems to be no good reason why the community should have to look to independent schools to provide a choice of approach in education."[10]

Forty years on, I am still in touch with over half of the Tagari students, thanks mainly to social media. They have taken on a variety of roles including Acting Commonwealth Ombudsman, Professor of Mathematics at Iowa State University, the only female Judge of the Supreme Court of Tasmania, two medical doctors, several teachers, horticulturalists, builders and financiers. One has built his own yacht and sailed the seven seas with his family. Most are now parents and grandparents. Many have continued interests and hobbies they started at Tagari – photography, sport, art and travel.

During the second Tagari year, the Commonwealth Government established a new organisation called the Curriculum Development Centre. While the government had stressed that the management of schools should rest with local communities in the states, it nevertheless acknowledged there was a need to support schools in developing guidelines that took account of the opportunities and challenges in rapidly changing times. The aim of the Curriculum Development Centre was not to develop specific curriculum elements, but rather to provide schools with information that would assist them in developing their own, often unique, response to changing circumstances.

Its Director was a prominent educator, Malcolm Skilbeck. He believed strongly in school based curriculum development. "I do not see the school as merely 'recipient' or 'vehicle' or 'adopter', but as partner and, often, initiator in the change process."[11]

In developing its policies, the CDC recognised that Australian communities had always varied greatly in their ethnicity, their geographic setting, their economic circumstances and their local cultures. Individual students within these settings had also varied widely in interests, abilities and family circumstances. Teachers traditionally saw the task of tailoring their programs to meet the needs of their individual students as a fundamental aspect of their professional role.

I was invited to take part in discussions about the best way to provide the necessary support. Skilbeck and his team decided to develop what they called a core curriculum for Australian schools. They were adamant that this core curriculum should not be a set of compulsory subjects. They believed that the teaching-learning processes, the learning situations, and the learning technologies were just as important as the subject matter. These could not be standardised. Rather, the core curriculum should be a set of continually updated values and intentions to guide schools as they met the challenges and opportunities of their unique communities within a changing world. Malcolm Skilbeck's belief that schools should be tasked with tailoring their courses to meet the needs of individuals and groups continued to be an essential part of our Tagari ethos. It was obvious to us that, even in a school of fifty students of roughly the same age, one size could not suit all. It is significant that, during the 1970s, a national agency such as the CDC saw classroom teachers among the experts needed to develop education policy.

At Tagari, we encouraged students to identify and choose the way they learnt best. Some chose to engage as much as possible in independent learning. Others were more comfortable being taught in a fairly structured way. We realised that some students were motivated by competition while others rejected competition as an incentive, choosing instead to maintain parity with their peers, the latter mainly from lower socio-economic backgrounds. I well remember the reactions of two girls who were struggling with an aspect of algebra. Marguerite's response was, "This stuff is stupid. I can't do it." Keryn's response was, "I must be stupid. I can't do it." My strategy for these two girls had to be responsive to their perceptions. Throughout the life of the Project, Fran and I were able to tailor our teaching to the learning needs of students as we came to know them well. These needs were not just about their prior learnings, but about their metacognition, about the way they learnt best.

In the second year of the Project, the Tasman Bridge was wrecked by the Lake Illawarra. About half the students lived on the eastern shore and half on the western shore of the Derwent. We had to adjust our teaching accordingly, because, for several months, it was not easy to have the group together. I set an individual research project for the science students now in their second high-school year. They could access libraries on either side of the river. In pairs, they were each to research a type of vertebrate animal ready to report back after a fortnight. David Stewart asked me if he could work on his own. I agreed, asking him what he wanted to research.

"I want to do sleep."

I thought he was joking. He wasn't.

"Vertebrates sleep," he said. "Why?"

I agreed that he could research sleep.

When he reported back to the full group, he hypothesised that the dinosaurs weren't really cold-blooded reptiles. His theory was that if an animal as large as T-Rex hibernated, its weight would destroy the tissues close to the ground on hibernation. The blood couldn't keep circulating to those tissues because the pressure of gravity would be greater than the animal's blood pressure.

"I've done the maths," the fourteen-year-old explained. Karen, one of the students, asked me what they should answer if there was an exam question about this. My reply was to say that most scientists believe the dinosaurs were reptiles but David Stewart, in our class, thinks they were more like birds.

Two years later, David came to school one morning waving a copy of *Scientific American*.

"They've found out," he beamed. Sure enough, the article described new research confirming that the dinosaurs had circulatory systems that were bird-like, and not cold- blooded. David is now professor of mathematics at Iowa State University.

About the time Tagari finished, an inspiring educator emerged onto the Australian education landscape. Garth Boomer was a contemporary of mine and I was pleased to call him a friend. He was a South Australian teacher and educator who was seen by many as the greatest influence on Australian teaching and teacher education in the 20th century. He began his career as a secondary teacher of English and mathematics in Adelaide and during his tragically short life he became Director of the Wattle Park Teachers Centre in South Australia (1980), and during the 1980s, Director of the National Curriculum Development Centre in Canberra and later Chairman of the Commonwealth Schools Commission. He died in 1993 of a brain tumour.

Whether he was working in the classroom or on national policies, Garth Boomer believed that learning needed to be collaborative – a partnership between teacher and students. He believed teachers should continually reflect on their teaching and make modifications as necessary. He saw teaching as action research that responded to the needs, interests and prior learnings of students. The details of curriculum development belonged to teachers.

The more richly a teacher can weave a tapestry of metaphor and analogy into a 'thick' redundant text of thinking about something new, the more likely that it is that students will find a way in.[12]

And from the famous book he edited called *Negotiating the Curriculum*,

"If teachers set out to teach according to a planned curriculum, without engaging the interests of the students, the quality of learning will suffer. … Negotiating the curriculum means deliberately planning to invite students to contribute to, and to modify, the educational program so that they will have a real investment both in the learning journey and in the outcomes."[13]

It doesn't take much reflection to realise that this kind of thinking fits a pattern. As soon as they are born, humans start learning. In their pre-school years, they are insatiable learners. Without formal or deliberate teaching, they learn to crawl, to walk, to talk. They do this best where there is a supportive and stimulating environment. Essentially, though, they learn because they choose to. They lift up rocks and taste things they sometimes shouldn't. They are fascinated by visual patterns and by the feel of textures. They decide what they want to do and what questions they will ask. The repeated question "Why?" is one that will resonate with many parents and grandparents.

For young children, learning is as natural as eating or sleeping. Boomer warned teachers against replacing this kind of learning with routines that forsook children's questions and replaced them with scripted answers to questions the children hadn't asked and that were created many miles away from their reality.

Of course, this does not mean keeping children in a bubble of their own environment; it means expanding the bubble in thoughtful ways, introducing them to new ideas and places so that new questions arise. Books and signs and objects raise questions that kids naturally want to know about. "What does that say?" "How many are there?" "How big is the fish you caught?" Reading, writing and figuring are tools to ask new questions and find new answers. Five-year-olds can appreciate this. Garth Boomer's influence on me and my contemporaries was profound. Leading politicians of the day were committed to educational excellence. They did not see education policy as the realm of politicians. This is evidenced by the Hawke government's appointment of Garth Boomer to chair the Commonwealth Schools Commission in 1985.

Chapter 5
Leaving Tasmania

Post Tagari, the 1980s was, for me, an almost unbelievable decade. In 1980, I was a deputy principal of a rural district school in Tasmania. In 1990, I was chairing Queensland's Ministerial Consultative Council on Curriculum. The journey from one to the other was a roller coaster.

When Tagari finished, I looked for an opportunity to test the idea of allowing different students to take varying amounts of time in achieving common learning outcomes. To me, it made no sense for students to progress through their schooling dependent only on the Earth's revolution around the sun. My thinking was stimulated by the kind of learning that happens outside schools. Pre-schoolers learn to crawl, walk, and talk off-schedule and at rates independent of their ultimate achievements. Formally, learning a musical instrument, little athletics, swimming, the scouting movement all accept the idea of a learning continuum. Students move from one 'grade' to the next, depending on what they achieve, not on how long they have been learning. A driver's licence is particularly powerful in critiquing the practice of standardising a learning program and using a norm-referenced approach to describe outcomes. We wouldn't dare give all student drivers twenty hours of driver education and send them out onto the roads with an A, B, C, D or E on their licence.

I undertook three kinds of professional activities. First, I wrote a book. It was called *Marking Time* (Methuen, 1982).[14] The title says it all. The book included case studies of alternative approaches to schooling and a critique of a system where children just had to enrol at school and wait until the Earth had orbited the Sun ten times in order to graduate.

Second, I began work on a post-graduate Masters Degree by thesis, an activity that was to turn my life upside down. I will return to this later in the chapter.

Third, I applied for a demotion to take charge of the secondary section of Sorell District School, a rural school outside Hobart where I believed I had a chance of putting into practice the exploration of alternative student pathways. I knew that learning any skill or concept requires variable time among groups of students. And the rate of learning is not constant for an individual. There are 'growth spurts' and 'down times.' Therefore, it is not just the total time that needs to vary. Variation also needs to happen along the way. And it needs to be possible between subject areas.

My earlier work on the Australian Science Education Project gave me clues as to how this might be achieved. The science project involved learning pathways where students undertook an initial learning activity. The resulting individualised pathway, and the time taken, depended on the ease with which they handled that activity and each subsequent activity. It seemed obvious to me that, if secondary school students were to be given the time they needed to progress, then any course would need to be divided into relatively small 'units', about thirty hours ideally. We decided on 'term' units in each subject. In 1980, there were three terms a year in Tasmania. We arranged that students would study six units in each term. This meant that each student would study eighteen units in total each year.

In maths, for example, until we made the change, every student would have to do three terms per year of maths (about five periods every week of the year), and therefore twelve units across years 7 to 10, no matter whether they were fast learners or slow learners. Once the change was made, students could do two, three or four units per year, depending on their speed of learning and their aspirations. This meant some might be able to achieve reasonable year 10 goals by studying just nine units, while others might need twelve or thirteen. The units were carefully sequenced to provide continuity. The pattern of units varied from subject to subject. Sometimes, it did not matter in which order students studied the separate units of a course in, say, the arts. However, in subjects such as mathematics, the sequence was planned to allow acceleration or consolidation. The sequence of units we developed was similar to the following.

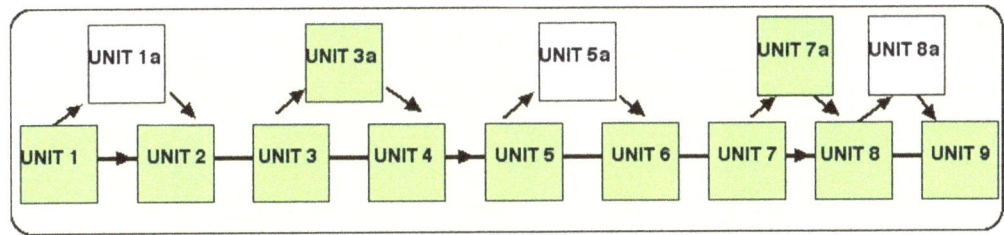

A very able and fast-learning student would have needed just the nine units shaded along the bottom row. The more complex shaded pattern, including 3a and 7a exemplifies a student who made reasonably good progress. However, after unit 3, in consultation with her maths teacher, she decided to pause and consolidate by choosing unit 3a. This allowed her to revise and master the goals of unit 3 and prepare well for unit 4. In all, she needed eleven units to complete the course, meaning there was just one term during her high school years when she didn't study maths. Other students, perhaps slower in learning, but highly aspirational, might have needed 13 units to achieve their goals meaning that for a term or so, they were studying two units of maths concurrently.

Because students were no longer grouped solely within year groups, this pattern of organisation came to be called 'vertical timetabling'.

As a result of my Tagari experience and the research needed for my book, *Marking Time*, I had developed networks across Australia and I learnt that a select committee of the NSW Legislative Council had come to the same conclusion I had. The resulting 1981 McGowan Report recommended the secondary school curriculum in NSW be based on semester units.[15] Brian McGowan, a member of the NSW Legislative Council, was an ex-Head of English at The Entrance High School. Schools began trialling this pattern over the next three years in both NSW and Queensland. During 1980 and 1981, I often travelled in NSW, Queensland and Tasmania assisting schools in implementing the pattern.

While this was occurring, I was attempting to complete a Tasmanian University Masters Research Degree about the origin of Matriculation Colleges in Tasmania. I was stimulated to do this because Professor Bill

Connell in his 1978 report to the Tasmanian government had written: "Despite the fact that Tasmania has the highest age for compulsory attendance of all States, 16 years, Tasmanian secondary education has the lowest holding power ... We wish to emphasise and recommend that continuity should be more clearly seen in the secondary program by planning a coordinated six-year curriculum, and by the addition of year 11 and 12 classes to some country and district high schools."[16]

I wondered why the new high schools of the 1950s and 1960s had not gone to years 11 and 12. Very early in my research, I was staggered to discover that the decision to introduce the year 11 and 12 Matriculation Colleges was the result of quite blatant corruption during the 1950s. I made the discovery as I went through the archives of the Tasmanian Teachers Federation. It is important to acknowledge that in the 1950s, the Teachers Federation was not considered a 'union' as we would interpret it today. It was made up of leading educators, many of whom were principals and teachers' college lecturers. In those days, it was the major advisory group to government.

My scanning of documents showed that motions passed at the 1954 annual conference of the Teachers Federation had been drastically altered in the conference report that was taken to the Minister for Education. I still have photocopies of the hand-written alterations that were made. There was a number of such alterations. However, two stand out. The first involved a motion to test support for the tripartite system that existed in Tasmania.

> Amendment.
> Moved by Mr. Bonner seconded Mr. Maslin.
> That the Federation is dissatisfied with the Tripartite System of Secondary Education in this state as it exists at present.
> Lost.

The motion was lost. However, the Report of the Conference to the Minister made the following recommendation.

> RECOMMENDATIONS.
>
> 1. Naturally, in a large service, there is not unanimity among members as to the best solution of these difficulties. However, after full debate the 1954 conference of the Federation gave support to the following principles:
>
> i. It is of profound importance that there should be no segregation of secondary school children on the lines of ability into separate schools.

The second alteration was even more blatant. It followed a discussion about Brooks Community School in a Launceston suburb. The future of the school was in question.

The motion put to the conference was as follows.

> Moved by Mr. Hudspeth seconded Mr. Childs.
>
> That this conference approves the establishment of a multilateral school such as that at Ulverstone.
>
> Carried.

I found the faded copy (altered by handwriting) passed to the typist who was preparing the report. (No computers in those days)

> ii. That this conference approves the establishment of ~~multilateral~~ schools such as that at Ulverstone. *comprehensive*

Note the additional 's' turning school into schools. The final Report to the Minister read as follows.

> In addition –
>
> Conference passed the following motions.
>
> That this conference approves the establishment of comprehensive schools such as that at Ulverstone.

As a result, instead of a minor recommendation affecting just Brooks Community School, the report recommended Tasmania shift immediately to a full-scale pattern of comprehensive schools. This was done – Clarence High, Taroona High, Newtown, Rose Bay, Parklands, Warrane, Queechy, Riverside, Cosgrove, Ogilvie, Kings Meadows, all within a decade. By 1961, it became apparent things had happened so quickly that 11 and 12 specialist staffing in all of these schools was not possible. Education Minister Bill Nielsen was faced with a dilemma. The only solution was to use the previous selective high schools, which did not have full technical facilities anyway, as Matriculation Colleges.

Educators who had been to the 1954 conference were staggered. Dwight Brown was one of these. In 1961, as headmaster of Hobart High School, he saw the last intake of year 7 students into his school. It was to become a Matriculation College. In that year, he wrote, "The change has come so rapidly. There is a breathlessness about the pace, a lack of objectivity about the opinions, and a hustle about the changes of plan that are not conducive to good educational practice."[17]

Later in the year, he wrote "…matriculation centralisation was intended to be an experiment at Hobart High School but we fear that before it can be fully assessed, and the real impact studied, there will be a similar college in Launceston. The thinking that these changes are experimental and they must succeed is highly dangerous because it prejudges the result."[17]

Brown's fears were well founded. Matriculation Colleges were quickly introduced in Launceston, Burnie and Devonport.

Fearing litigation, the university would not let me use my research at the time (although later, a new faculty Dean, Phillip Hughes, granted my Masters). In May of 1980, I approached Bruce Poulson of the Historical Society to get my work published independently. Bruce must have discussed the research with others. His decision to do this changed my life.

One wintry May evening in 1980, two very senior members of the Education Department who, 26 years earlier, had been the minute secretaries for the 1954 Conference, came to my family home, unannounced, and told me I had no future in Tasmania if I made my research public. I asked why.

"The research is correct. Someone altered the minutes of the 1954 Conference when the Report was presented to the Minister."

The reply staggered me.

"I know. It was me. It's the job of the minute secretary to clarify the wording of motions."

"But you moved the motion in the first place," I argued.

He shrugged his shoulders and added that I had no proof that the Report actually went to the Minister. His colleague, whom I realised was not involved in the deception, took some papers from a briefcase and scanned one of the documents.

"It did go to the Minister," he said, "According to the executive minutes, you took the Report to him personally."

The two now seemed at odds with each other. They left abruptly and I was left in limbo.

Over the following months, I continued to work on the vertical curriculum at Sorell and to participate by invitation in conferences and consultancies on the 'mainland', including work with the Commonwealth Schools Commission and with the Curriculum Development Centre as the latter developed its Core Curriculum for Australian Schools. While I did not go out of my way to be critical of Tasmania's Senior College system, I was nevertheless aware of some of the failings of the pattern. The retention rates into years 11 and 12 were the lowest of Australian states. The youth unemployment rate was high. So was the youth crime rate. Country kids could only study years 11 and 12 if their parents were prepared to move to one of the four main cities in the state, or if they were prepared, financially and socially, to board away from home. The pattern was clearly inequitable; less wealthy country people had no access.

The matter came to a head for me in 1982 at a national Schools Commission Conference at Lorne in Victoria. I was not an official delegate from Tasmania. I had been invited as a guest speaker. On the final afternoon of the Conference, there was to be a panel discussion. Joan Kirner, who was organising the program, asked me at morning tea if I was prepared to join the panel that consisted mainly of state delegates. She believed there would be no fruitful debate if the panel was made up of cautious state bureaucrats. I agreed. At lunch time, Tasmania's delegate, the Deputy Director General of Education, approached me.

"I hear you are on the panel."

"Yes," I replied.

"Well you and I should agree on things. Otherwise it will look bad for Tasmania. Is that OK with you?"

I laughed, taking it lightly. He obviously wasn't amused.

"You will agree with me then?"

"I haven't heard what you've said yet," I replied, again in good humour, I thought.

There was no significant discussion about Tasmania during the panel session. However, shortly after this conference, I received a letter from Tasmania's Director-General of Education. "While I am Director-General, you will not leave this state on professional matters."

So began another chapter of my life.

Chapter 6
Queensland and South Australia

It was obvious I needed to resign from the Tasmanian Education Department and continue my career elsewhere, despite my son Leigh being just one month old and despite my having just bought a house on Hobart's Eastern Shore. I had already undertaken a major consultancy in Queensland during 1982 and I was urged to accept a full year consultancy for 1983. This was based in Brisbane and was sponsored by the Queensland Inter-Systemic Parents Council (QIPC). It was an attractive proposition, and I had no hesitation in accepting it.

The year expanded my experience immensely. The Council represented parents from Catholic, State, and Independent schools as well as the Isolated Children's Parents Association (ICPA). Although most of my engagements were in South East Queensland, I had the privilege of working with school communities (parents, teachers and students) in all areas of the state from Cairns in the north to Birdsville and Cunnamulla in the outback. The work varied from creating school timetables to speaking at conferences and consulting with parent groups. I found myself working in primary schools much more than I had done in the past, taking part in many conferences involving principals and school administrators as well as parent organisations.

In March of 1983, Labor's Bob Hawke won the Federal Election. This had major impacts on Australian education and provided educators like me with extra opportunities. Hawke helped shape Australian identity in a populist way. Within six months of his election win in March 1983, the yacht Australia II won the America's Cup in Newport, Rhode Island, a win that he famously championed on the morning of the victory when he stated that, "Any boss who sacks anyone for not turning up today is a bum." In April 1984, "Advance Australia Fair" finally became Australia's national anthem.

During the early 1980s, global advances in technology had been catalysts for unprecedented changes in politics, education, employment and in the day to day lives of Australians. In 1982, Barry Jones had alerted Australians to the transformations in his book *Sleepers Wake!: Technology and the Future of Work*.[18] An ex-high school teacher, Jones had been a member of the Victorian Parliament before becoming Federal Science Minister in 1983, a position he held until 1992. As Science Minister, Jones highlighted the way underlying historical advances in technology had affected the long-term lives of humans more than the more spectacular wars, explorations and social revolutions. He drew attention to revolutions such as the agrarian revolution and the industrial revolution. His accurate prediction that Australian manufacturing would progressively give way to information-based industries had a major effect on education policy. Central authorities, such as state and federal governments, provided new parameters and funding mechanisms to support schools as they introduced 'work experience' and 'transition education' programs. There were also challenges in providing new technologies. During the next decade, Australia experienced the widespread introduction of personal computers, faxes, emails and access to the internet. All Australians felt the change. *Marking Time*,[14] my book published in 1982, was written on a manual typewriter. *Making the Future*,[19] a book I co-authored in 1986, was written on a computer. People working at the federal and state levels and in schools could not ignore the social and industrial changes that were occurring.

Hawke's experience as President of the ACTU helped him design an Accord between the Labor Government and the unions. The agreement was that the unions would stop seeking continuous wage increases and in return the government would provide a 'social wage' and would involve unions in policy making. The Accord was signed in 1983. In 1984, the separate state teachers' federations combined to form the Australian Teachers Union. This move changed the nature of the state federations, causing them to focus much more on wages and conditions than on policy making and advice to governments within their own states. While this move to a national union may have had industrial benefits, it later had unintended and unfortunate consequences for Australian education as we shall see in Chapter 13.

During 1983, my belief that students should have the time needed for their learning to be effective remained a passion. The advent of the Hawke government provided me with a new set of possibilities. I applied to the newly formed Australian Department of Education and Youth Affairs for funding to support a 'Project of National Significance'. The project was designed to create a network among secondary schools across the nation that were implementing vertical curriculum patterns and to organise a national conference in 1984 bringing together curriculum leaders from these schools. The application was successful. The parents' council was fully supportive. I consulted in a number of Queensland schools that were already exploring the potential. It was significant that schools across the nation at that time were free to create these flexible patterns of student progression because the subject syllabuses provided the freedom for teachers to develop programs that were not based on year levels. In 1983, there were vertically timetabled schools in every state and in the Northern Territory.

Towards the end of 1983, I had to decide on my plans for the following years. I hankered to work in a school that would benefit from flexible learning patterns. I noticed that the South Australian Education Department was advertising contractual 'super-principal' positions in four high schools in and around Adelaide. My experience of South Australian education was limited. I had written a case study on the innovative Burra Community School which formed a chapter in my book *Marking Time*. In 1982, I had worked in partnership with Chris McCabe, who had been the inaugural principal at Burra, on a three-week consultancy in Queensland. I had also met John Steinle, the state's Director-General of Education, at several national conferences and through him, I knew that, under Premier Don Dunston, South Australia was an innovative state as far as education was concerned. I had nothing to lose by applying.

Things didn't start well. At short notice, I was contacted and asked to fly to Adelaide for an interview. I phoned Chris McCabe and arranged to stay with him for the two nights I would need in Adelaide. The day of my flight was very hot in Brisbane. I packed my suit in a case and flew to Adelaide in shorts and a T-shirt. Alas, my luggage was lost somewhere in transit and my interview was early the next day. I had to decide whether to attend in shorts and T-shirt or to borrow clothes from Chris. We decided on the latter. However, Chris is a bigger man than me. I'm afraid I looked rather like Charlie Chaplin as I fronted up to the interview panel. I explained the situation to the panel and their amusement got the interview off to a friendly start.

As it turned out, I was appointed principal of Elizabeth West High School from term 1, 1984. During the school holidays, I found a house to rent and moved to Adelaide with my wife and two toddlers, aged 1 and 3. Elizabeth is a satellite city of Adelaide. It was planned and constructed in the 1950s and attracted a large population of British migrants into the public housing estates. They were joined by many Aboriginal families. By the 1980s, the population was ageing and the number of students at Elizabeth West High School had been declining for some time. The enrolment was down to around 400 students.

On arriving at the school prior to the first day of term, I found the physical environment of the school to be depressing. In terms of buildings, it was a large school, designed for far more students than were enrolled. However, I was impressed by the quality and dedication of the teaching staff. My early life as principal there involved some embarrassing episodes. For example, at the first school assembly, I introduced myself and then proceeded to introduce the new teachers for 1984. One of these was an attractive young woman who was welcomed by several 'wolf whistles'. Determined to assert my authority, I responded by telling the group that there were more appropriate ways of expressing their appreciation.

"Well how would you do it Sir?" was the call from the back row.

I learnt quickly to think carefully before taking these kids on. At the same time, I appreciated their pluck.

At the first principals' conference, I was welcomed as "Mike Middleton, the first of what we hope is not a long list of immigrants." The comment was light-hearted. But I understood the nuance. In retrospect, I suspect there were not a lot of applicants from South Australians for Elizabeth West. My three years at Elizabeth West were a mixture of positives and negatives. Partly because of circumstances and partly because of my own naivety and inexperience, I think the negatives probably outweighed the positives. We'll scan the positives first.

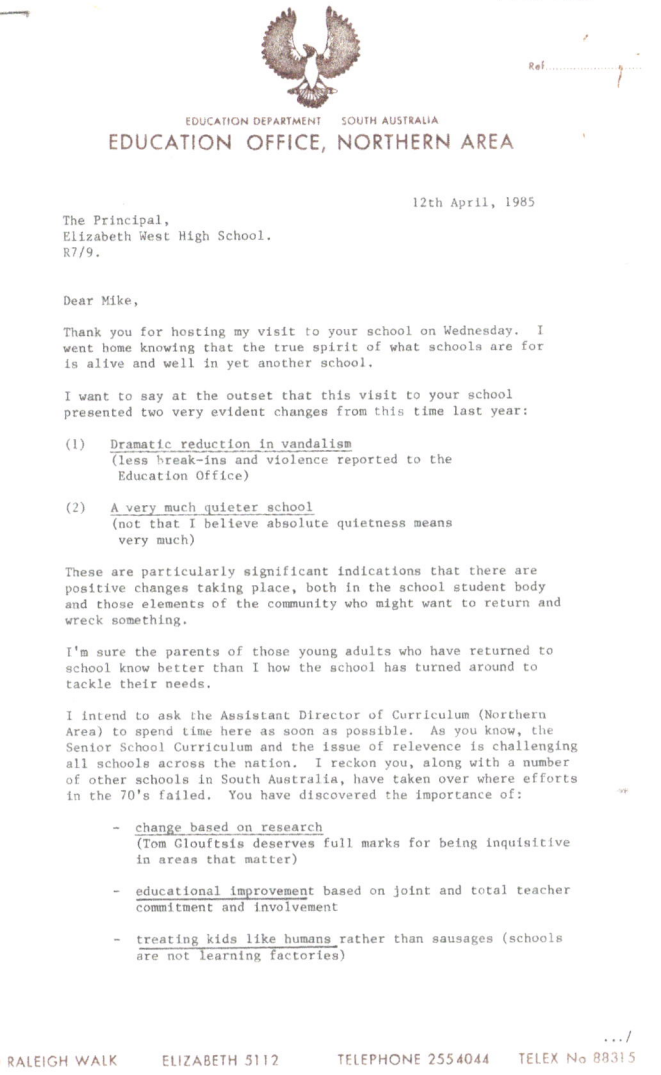

An early challenge was to tackle the physical environment. The ground staff did their best, but there was a lot of graffiti on the school's internal and external walls. I decided that the best way to tackle the problem might be to get the kids choosing colours and patterns and painting walls, starting in the corridors. I wasn't sure that I was allowed to do this. I wrote a letter to Regional Office to the effect that, if they did not say 'no', I was arranging to repaint the walls of the corridors and rooms. I took no reply to mean 'yes'. Teachers who knew the students well chose working groups of assertive kids to do the painting. It worked. The kids took pride in their paintwork and discouraged any would-be vandals. We expanded the program to include some other structures in the school grounds. The maintenance costs began to fall.

I was able to work with middle managers in creating a flexible curriculum pattern based on term length units. The school's enrolment had been falling for some years. However, there were hundreds of single mothers in Elizabeth, many of them teenagers. The school had an excess of facilities and rooms. By converting one of the Home Economics areas into a childcare centre, we were able to encourage mothers to return and continue their studies.

The flexible curriculum pattern really helped because the mothers could engage in subjects based on their previous achievements or lack thereof. And their commitment was ten weeks at a time, and part-time if necessary. The program proved to be popular and dozens of women re-entered schooling as a result. However, after some months, the local council got wind of the program and advised me that the child care centre was not 'legal' because it had not gone through the appropriate processes. I had the task, at morning tea one day, of advising the mothers that we would have to discontinue the program. They were not happy.

"We'll see about that," one of them said angrily. I wondered what that meant.

At lunch time that day, I had a telephone call.

"This is the Ray Martin Midday show. We are coming to Elizabeth to make a program about your childcare centre."

"We don't have a childcare centre anymore."

"We know. That's what the program will be about. We'll be there on Monday."

I was taken aback. Clearly, the mothers had taken action that had immediate results.

"Leave it with me."

I phoned the Regional Office seeking advice. They said they would call me back, which they did about ten minutes later.

"The Minister says can you put them off till early next year. By then, we should be able to get it okayed."

I phoned the producer back suggesting they delay their visit until next year when the centre should be up and operating again.

"No. As I said, we'll be there on Monday."

"What if I say you can't come onto the property?"

"That will make the best program of all."

I phoned Regional Office again, explaining the situation.

"Oh no! I'll get back to you."

About half an hour later, I received a call.

"You have thirty-five thousand dollars to convert the facility and we will fast track it for you. Keep it open. We will negotiate with the Council."

A crew from the Midday Show did come on the Monday. The reporter, George, was sensitive to what we were doing. The segment was very supportive.

Steve Cox was an excellent Welfare Officer who drew my attention to the fact that there were also hundreds of male 'street kids' in Elizabeth, many of whom had either dropped out of school or been expelled. We had a program for young mothers. What about young men?

We devised a plan to encourage them back to school. Steve would go to the shopping centres and railway stations and spread the word that on Tuesday afternoons, boys could come back to one of the demountable buildings called the Kabbarli and talk about the possibilities. I chose to be there each Tuesday. On the second Tuesday, a boy called Trevor fronted up. I knew him by reputation as a leader in the neighbourhood.

"Come in Trevor. Do you want a cup of coffee?"

"Nup."

"Do you want to take a seat?

"Nup." He stood with his hands on his hips.

"Can youse learn me how to read and write without anyone knowing what you're doing?"

I hesitated, trying to process the question. Trevor looked impatient.

"Sure," I said unsurely.

"Well I'm back and so are me mates." His eye contact and tone of voice were vaguely threatening. Steve joined him and they filled out some forms and made arrangements for 'mates' to do the same.

At first, the initiative (and the initiator) was unpopular among some of the teachers. A number of the boys had been expelled previously. They were a motley lot. Teachers in areas like woodwork, home economics, metalwork, drama, art and music were happy to have them back. It didn't take long, however, for teachers in science, English and maths to ask for these students to join their classes. Because they were finally motivated, these re-entry students improved the general discipline and culture in the classes, even if it involved threats to the younger students if they 'mucked up'.

These were positive aspects of my involvement in the school. However, there were issues that detracted from the effectiveness of my role as principal. In the first year, because of the Project of National Significance that I was still administering, a number of visitors from other schools came to talk with me about their programs and about the organisation of the national conference that was held mid-year in Sydney. There were also requests for me to spend time in other schools and school communities and as a conference speaker. This accelerated in the next two years. These were not private consultancies and initially I saw them as part of my job as a 'class A principal'. Some of them I could not refuse in any case because they were made through the hierarchy of the Education Department. For example, the Western Australian Beazley Report was released during 1984 and the South Australian Department was asked to release me for a week to introduce WA principals to the concepts involved in vertical timetabling. Director General John Steinle received a letter from his Western Australian counterpart.

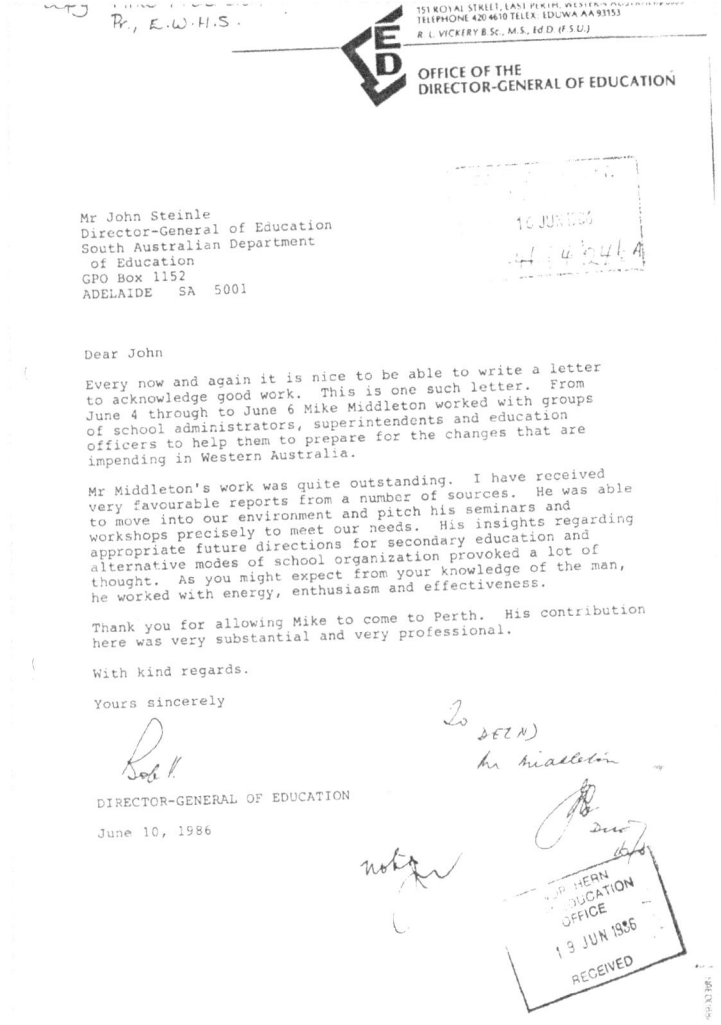

In the 1980s, the Catholic system in New Zealand was being integrated into the government system and I was asked to go to Wellington to help reassure the Catholic principals that they could timetable their schools so that integration did not mean they would lose their Catholic identity, and their religious education programs, in the process.

I also had requests from the Northern Territory, from Queensland and NSW and from many schools in South Australia. I found myself caught between a rock and a hard place. I welcomed the chance to make a difference beyond my own school and I considered it to be a legitimate part of my role. I was also aware of the need to be part of the team in my school. I sometimes involved teachers from Elizabeth West in my visits to other places, and a number of them attended the National 'Projects of National Significance' conference I led mid-year in Sydney in 1984.

I made arrangements with the teaching staff that if any of them were, for personal or social reasons, spending weekends visiting other places in South Australia or interstate, they should let me know. Where there were interesting schools in those places, I would provide two or three relief days so that they could visit these schools and bring ideas back. By my third year, I was aware of the dangers of my engagements away from the school and I tried to limit external involvements. That this was not effective is obvious. In writing this chapter, I decided to review the diaries I kept at the time. In retrospect, I wonder how I coped. My diary for April 1986 was fairly typical.

APRIL 1986	APRIL 1986	APRIL 1986	APRIL/MAY 1986
Mon 7th Eliz West	Mon 14th NSW P's Conference	Mon 21st Eliz West	Mon 28th Sydney Conference
Tues 8th (Coffs Harb., Princ Conference)	Tue 15th NSW P's Conference	Tues 22nd Eliz West	Tues 29th Bathurst Conference
Wed 9th (Coffs Harb, " ")	Wed 16th Victor Harbour Cath Ed Off	Wed 23rd Peterborough H S	Wed 30th Sydney Conference
Thu 10th Towoomba Princ Conference	Th 17th Eliz West	Thu 24th Fly to New Zealand	Thu May 1st Eliz West
Fri 11th Toowoomba " "	Fri 18th Eliz West	Fri 25th NZ Catholic Principals	Fri May 2nd Meeting with J Steinle
Sat 12th ADELAIDE		Sat 26th NZ Catholic Principals	
Sun 13th to Robertson NSW		Sun 27th NZ Catholic Principals	

I now realise that my continuing engagements were at odds with what I was trying to communicate – a commitment to one's own school – and it was an unintended form of hypocrisy.

The problem was compounded when the Director General, John Steinle, requested that I be seconded to the Commonwealth Schools Commission for some weeks to lead a team of four writers, representative of SA, NSW, Queensland and Victoria, in developing a discussion paper about the future of secondary schooling in Australia. Steinle had recently visited the school and was impressed with what he saw. What he didn't appreciate was my continuing dilemma.

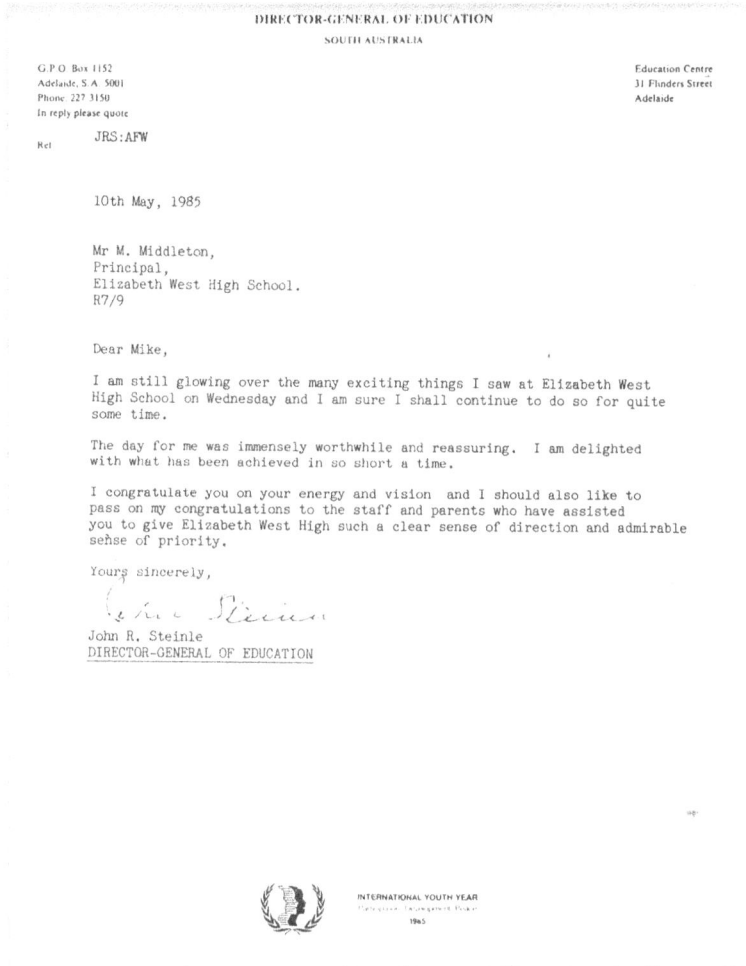

The plan was that, unless I was meeting with the co-authors, I would stay based at Elizabeth West, but would hand over the job of principal to the deputy during the period it took to write the discussion paper.

The next few months were negative for two reasons. First, the Schools Commission did not provide clear expectations for the writing team. We struggled to interpret our task. We felt pressure to tackle the issue of equity in secondary education and two of the writing team were very strong advocates for this to be the major thrust of the discussion paper. However, in retrospect, I believe the Commission's main hope was that the paper would tackle the practical issues of curriculum and school structures. Consequently, the book *(Making the Future: The Role of Secondary Education in Australia – Schools Commission 1986)*[19] turned out to be much more a statement about the need for equity than it was a statement about how to improve the quality of secondary education. The book was read and appreciated by academics. However, I suspect very few school-based people read it.

Second, it was difficult to be in a school where I was substantively the principal but had appointed a deputy to take on the role. I remember being in staff meetings where teachers would turn to me for an answer, but I had to indicate that I was not the person to make the decision. In hindsight, it would have been better for me to be away from the school during this time.

When I returned to the principal's role, I found it difficult to re-engage. The school was at a tipping point. The intake from the local primary schools had all but dried up. The fact that we were taking on re-entry students probably discouraged some parents of primary school children. What would the school be? Would it continue as a traditional high school? This option was problematic, given the number of re-entry students already enrolled. Should it become a re-entry college? I was aware of Tuart and Canning Colleges in Western Australia and the way they had evolved from more traditional high schools. I drew the staff's attention to these examples.

As it turned out, the answers to these questions were not mine to provide. The stresses of the job were exacerbated by some of the judgements I had to make in trying to satisfy conflicting day-to-day demands. The issue came to a head one day when a year 11 boy in the canteen queue turned around and 'king hit' the year 12 boy behind him. An ambulance was called and the victim was taken to hospital. There was widespread pressure from staff and at least some students to punish the assailant by expulsion and/or legal action. I looked at the year 11 boy's record. I will call him Peter. There was no hint of any previous misbehaviour, let alone violence. I sat him in my office and asked him why he had taken the action he had. He was tight-lipped and would not answer. He just shook his head. I had a sense that there was more to it than a sudden urge to hit someone.

After an hour or so of my coming and going, he realised that I was not going to give up in a hurry.

"If I tell you, will you promise not to tell anyone?"

"I'll do whatever I can."

He told me his story. His mum was single and there were younger siblings. She was in financial trouble and had used some limited episodes of late-night home-based prostitution to support her family. As Peter bought a lunch time pie at the canteen, the boy behind said "I paid for that."

I called the Department of Child Protection and they came and picked Peter up. This took the matter out of my hands. The episode was one of the catalysts for me to take leave and consider my future.

I was aware that the nature of my work had not been ideal for my wife and young family. My daughter Ariane was six years old. Son Leigh, aged three, had already lived in six houses in three states. The contract at Elizabeth West was for five years, so I would, in any case, be relocating to a new position somewhere by 1988. We decided to return to Brisbane.

At the time, Australian education was in a state of flux. Internally, it was alive with initiatives that were meeting the opportunities and challenges of a rapidly changing world. In NSW, the 1981 McGowan Report had provided a stimulus for Government, Catholic and Independent secondary schools to explore ways of supporting students who had different learning rates. The Western Australian Beazley Report of 1984[21] had recommended schools in that state explore the possibilities of vertical timetabling. While there were no specific reports recommending such explorations in South Australia, Victoria and the Northern Territory, there was nevertheless a number of schools including Huntingdale Tech in Victoria and Sanderson High School in Darwin that were developing continuous learning patterns for students.

The Queensland population was increasing rapidly and new schools like Craigslea High School in Brisbane and Burnside High School in Nambour were taking advantage of innovative architectural designs to create more continuous and integrated programs, including 'year 8 centres', the forerunners of middle schools. Runcorn High School in Brisbane and St John's Catholic School in Nambour were among the Queensland schools that had developed fully vertical timetable patterns. I figured that Queensland had exciting potential for me if I could find the right niche.

The external factors impinging on schooling were changing, reflecting the broader social changes that were predicted by Barry Jones in his 1982 book, *Sleepers Wake*.

Paul Keating's famous 'banana republic' comment was made in May 1986 from a restaurant wall telephone to the John Laws' morning radio program. Part of his conversation reflected the government's concern about Australia's economic future.

"In the 1970s, we became a third world economy selling raw materials and food and we let the sophisticated industrial side fall apart. … If this government cannot get … manufacturing going again and keep moderate wage outcomes and a sensible economic policy, then Australia is basically done for. We will just end up being a third-rate economy, a banana republic."

The patterns of employment were shifting towards white collar service industries requiring higher levels of education. The country was changing from a situation where there was a shortage of labour to one where unemployment was becoming an issue. The Australian Bureau of Statistics records that between 1945 and 1965, the average unemployment rate was 2 per cent. Between 1965 and 1985, that average had risen to 7.5 per cent. As a result, schools were seeking ways to accommodate programs of 'vocational education.' The situation clearly required proactive approaches to timetabling.

Chapter 7
A Tertiary Role

When I returned to Queensland with my family, I canvassed the professional options available. I contacted three prospective employers. The first was the Queensland Education Department. Their policy was that anyone joining their service from outside would start as a classroom teacher. The Catholic Education Office was much more encouraging. Despite my not being Catholic, they talked with me about a deputy principal's role in one of their colleges. The Mount Gravatt campus of the Brisbane College of Advanced Education offered me a role as lecturer in education.

Reflecting on my skills and my goals, I realised that I was, above all, a teacher, a person who liked to find ways of communicating possibilities and ideas, whether it be with students, educators, parents or business people. Elizabeth West High School had been frustrating because I was less passionate about my administrative role than I was about my broader role as a communicator and change agent. I had allowed my time commitment to the school to be reduced to the point where the administrative role suffered. I concluded that I needed a role that afforded me the flexibility to continue networking and pursuing new ideas. Only the lecturing position at Mt Gravatt would provide this.

That is how it turned out. The Mount Gravatt campus of the Brisbane College of Advanced Education (which was to become part of Griffith

University in 1990) encouraged outside professional engagements and gave its lecturers at least a day a week to facilitate such involvement. The formal teaching load was modest, involving about three or four courses, each having two hour-long lectures and three tutorials per week. This left time for writing, for research and for consulting or speaking engagements.

For the first ten of my twenty years in Queensland, lecturing was the constant 'base rhythm' of my life. A range of other professional activities provided the melody. Nevertheless, I did appreciate the continuity of relationships and routines involved in my work at the university. I enjoyed the camaraderie with colleagues and I met many interesting students. There wasn't a lot of room for risk-taking or innovation. The culture was such that any new idea was a challenge for academics who revelled in telling you why it wouldn't work. I tried to encourage a pattern of internships where lecturers would work with teachers in schools to develop on-the-job programs for final year teacher education students. But academia was more about abstract ideals than it was about the rough and tumble of classrooms.

My one episode of risk-taking, late in my time at Griffith, involved a class of post-graduates who were a lively bunch of about forty students. I was taking a semester unit titled "Co-operative Assessment and Evaluation". At the first lecture, one of the students asked a provocative question.

"If this unit is about co-operative evaluation, can we collaborate and share the same grade at the end of semester?"

I treated the question lightly. "That would only be possible if all of you agreed."

I thought no more about it until the second lecture when a student raised her hand and said, "Before we get started, can we test the response to our request to share the same grade?"

I was taken aback, but still confident of my intuition. "OK, stand up all those who are prepared to share the same grade at the end of semester."

They had obviously caucused. Everyone stood up.

"Is everyone here?" I asked in desperation.

"All here," the young woman said.

I counted the group.

"Well?"

"Let's do it," I said. "But every one of you will have to pull your weight."

"We'll make sure of that."

Thus began an enlightening experience. Every lecture and tutorial, students arrived with handouts for other students. They all turned up to lectures and tutorials and participated fully. I was amazed. The 'normal' situation where the success of some students depended on the relative failure of others no longer applied. There would be no 'normal' curve. Instead of students competing for grades, they were sharing information and insights to elevate their shared grade. Assessment involved seminar presentations and written assignments that were co-authored. I arranged that the final assessment 'exam' was such that they could answer in groups and seek advice from other groups. Never had I worked with such an enthusiastic and professional group.

At the final lecture, we negotiated the grade. The general consensus was that the award should be a 'six'. This was, in lay terms, a distinction, one grade below 7 which was the maximum high distinction. I dutifully transmitted the results to the faculty office. Almost immediately, I received a call from the data entry person recording the grades.

"Hey Mike, something's gone awry with the computer program. All the students are showing a 'six'."

"Yeah, that's correct," I replied.

There was a long pause.

"Oh. … Thanks"

I knew it was coming. I got a call from the faculty dean asking me to his office.

"You can't do this," he said. "Haven't you read the guidelines?"

I tried to explain to him what had happened and that this was the most engaged and able group of students I had ever been involved with. He shook his head.

"We are going to have to let it stand. But don't ever do this again."

An intensive but fairly short-lived activity commenced in December 1988. Brian Littleproud had been appointed Queensland's Minister for Education in December of the previous year. He was a member of Joh Bjelke-Petersen's Cabinet and had an office in the Education Department building. One day in the spring of 1988, I came across Brian in the elevator. We had talked casually before. He said hello and shook my hand.

"I've been wanting to talk with you," he said. "I want you to chair my Council. Could you come to my office tomorrow? Make a time with my receptionist."

Next day, he welcomed me into his office and arranged a cup of tea for both of us. He explained that he was introducing legislation setting up a statutory council to consult with Queenslanders about their views on priorities for the state's curriculum. He wanted me to chair the council which was to be called the Ministerial Consultative Council on Curriculum (MCCC). I'd always considered myself a bit of a leftie. I had heard much about the alleged 'cronyism' in the Bjelke-Petersen Government and I started to explain that I wasn't politically aligned. He stopped me immediately and said that he was not interested in my politics. He was interested in my knowledge and skill as an educator and a communicator.

As we talked, I realised that his agenda was not political either. He genuinely wanted to find out what young people would need to know and be able to do if they were to be active future citizens. I was impressed then with Brian Littleproud and nothing since has caused me to change my opinion of him.

Members of the MCCC included administrators, teachers and parents from Catholic, State and Independent schools along with representatives from tertiary education. It was a privilege to work with these people and with the wonderful writers and consultants we contracted to undertake the research. As was its charter, the Council set up working parties to survey and consult with a range of community groups about their views on what should be taught in schools, and how. These included, in turn, groups of teachers, administrators, citizens, migrants, first nations people and members of key organisations such as the CWA, YMCA, churches, businesses and environmental groups.

The Council also commissioned a number of discussion papers about educational issues. These were written by experts in their field. The writers addressed issues such as The New Basics, Early Childhood Education, Asian Studies, Future Needs in Education, the Importance of Consultation, and Oracy (an often-overlooked skill).

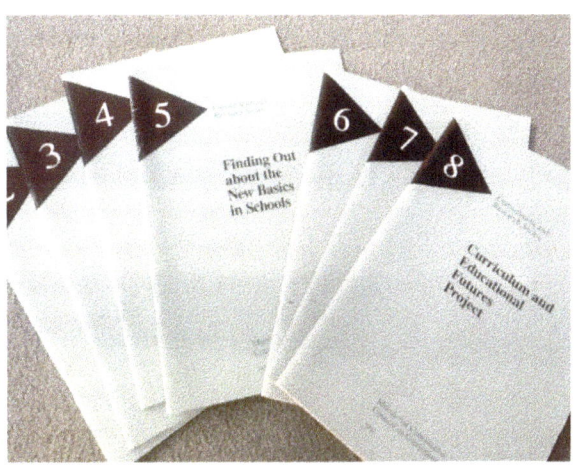

As chair of the Council, I was frequently interviewed on local ABC radio about these emerging issues. Interestingly, the concept of 'new basics' was one of the issues discussed as early as 1989.[20] The photograph below records a discussion with Education Minister Brian Littleproud in 1989 about the need to explore the new basics concept.

There were some trivial, sometimes embarrassing, events associated with my role as Council chair. In 1989, I attended the annual conference in Cairns of the Queensland Council of Parents and Citizens Association as a guest speaker. The conference was to be opened by Education Minister Brian Littleproud. However, on the morning of the Conference, Brian phoned me explaining that Parliament had been called and would I open the Conference on his behalf? This threw me a little. I hastily crafted a speech and dressed in a suit and tie, arriving at the Cairns Council venue with five minutes to spare. I was stopped at the entrance by a member

of the Cairns Council who told me that I was inappropriately dressed to attend the Conference. He was unaware that I was the Minister's replacement. I'm not sure it would have made any difference if he had been aware. I began to question his judgement. But he interrupted. saying that it was Council policy that no one was allowed to wear a tie in the hot and humid climate of Cairns because it lowered productivity. I removed my coat and tie and opened the Conference in rolled-up shirt sleeves.

On 7th December 1989, the Labor Party, under Wayne Goss, won the state election. The Council continued to function for a further three years under two Labor Education Ministers. I was not convinced that they were apolitically interested in what Queenslanders were saying about the appropriate learning for students in schools. Perhaps they were not keen to support an initiative created by the National Party. The Council was disbanded in 1992. However, the concept of 'new basics' continued to be developed as a formal project for the next fifteen years.

Chapter 8
Self-Employment Adventures

When the Ministerial Council was disbanded, the demands on my time did not diminish. I could not do justice to a full lecturing load and I arranged with Mary-Anne Fulton, a long-time friend and colleague, to share my university lecturing load 50-50 so that I had more time available for consulting work. After two years, even this did not provide enough flexibility and I resigned my lectureship at Griffith University.

In 1997, I felt the need to renew my classroom teaching experience. I took a relief teaching position for a term at St Aidan's Girls School in Brisbane, a school that had adopted a vertical timetable pattern. I needed this experience to keep me 'grounded'. It did that.

I continued to be committed to the need for our schools and school systems to be responsive to the changes occurring in society generally, and in the nature of work in particular. If teachers in schools were to do this effectively, they needed the freedom and encouragement to explore new ways of designing learning programs to meet the needs of particular communities as the world changed around them. They also needed ways of networking so the successes could be shared and the whole community of schools could advance by learning from each other. I teamed up with a NSW colleague, Jennifer Hill, to write a book called *Changing Schools* that was published in 1998.[38] This book stressed the importance of school autonomy and the professional role of teachers in creating learning programs that were continuously adaptable to the rapid changes occurring in communities.

In 1991, the Australian Children's Television Foundation launched a television series titled "Lift Off". Prior to the development of the series, I had been invited to take part in two workshops designed to brainstorm ideas for the programs. One of these workshops was in Lorne and the other in Warburton, Victoria. The ACTF director, Patricia Edgar, invited people from a wide range of backgrounds including chefs, artists, business people, technicians and educators. A highlight for me was engaging again with Garth Boomer who was also a participant in the workshops.

As the series was launched, I was asked to lead a team to publicise the Lift Off series in Queensland. We arranged a Lift Off bus to tour the state. I was invited onto the Board of the ACTF which met regularly in Melbourne. Other members of the board included Patricia Edgar, Janet Holmes à Court, Steve Vizard, Hazel Hawke and Graeme Foster, a colleague from Tasmania. While I enjoyed working on the Board and meeting these people, I was not suited to the role because my networks were with educationalists, rather than influential people who were able to generate sponsorship and financial support. I left the Board after a couple of years.

The work with the Ministerial Council had involved me in networks among Government, Catholic and Lutheran schools, not just in Queensland, but in other states too. As the 20th century was drawing to a close, the leaders of the Lutheran School System were keen to assess its progress in Australia. I was asked to undertake a detailed review involving me in visits to all Lutheran schools in Australia, the majority of which are in South Australia and Queensland. This work, which took several months, was extremely enjoyable because it involved interactions with students, teachers and parents in local communities. The resulting report was released at a major conference on the Gold Coast.[22]

One episode during this consultancy was quite embarrassing. I was working at a Lutheran school in Kingaroy, and enjoyed very much the discussions and camaraderie I shared with the principal, Helen Folker. At the end of the week, prior to my driving back to my home in Brisbane, she suggested that we review the week over a cup of coffee. During the conversation, I made a light-hearted remark.

"Kingaroy is a pretty notorious place. Does old Joh still live here?"

Her eyes sparkled a mischief.

"Yeah, Dad's still here."

My mind raced. What have I said all week? She appreciated my embarrassment and laughed. I wondered, if Joh Bjelke-Petersen was all that he was reputed to be, how could he have such an insightful daughter whose beliefs about multiculturalism and the environment were so enlightened? I still wonder.

A very interesting consultancy occurred when I was contacted by an international school in Hong Kong. Because of the SARS epidemic, their students were not able to attend school for some months and had to work from home. The leaders of the school were very concerned about the effect this would have on students' results in the International Baccalaureate. As it turned out, the student results improved markedly. I was engaged to find out why this had occurred and then to help the school incorporate the apparent advantages of home schooling into its classroom-based program. I had several trips to Hong Kong during which I realised that the way the Cantonese language characters were taught involved a very teacher-directed rote learning approach. This approach had spilled over into other subjects so that most student learning depended on being taught.

To some extent, this phenomenon was familiar to me because of my experience as a lecturer. I had found that the students who came to the university from outback properties where much of their schooling was through distance education were much more proactive and independent than many of those who had come directly from year 12 in secondary schools. I was able to help the Hong Kong school adjust its programs to give students opportunities for autonomous learning. Later, I was asked back to help include Mandarin in the school curriculum as it was mandated by the Chinese take-over of Hong Kong.

One amusing, but scary, aspect of my work in Hong Kong was the presence of 'bodyguards' in primary school classrooms. A small number of students were from rich families who feared their children might be kidnapped for ransom. The sight of dark-suited men with sunglasses sitting quietly and poker-faced at the back of some primary classrooms was amusing but disturbing at the same time.

The 1987 stock market crash and the ensuing recession had a significant impact on communities in western Queensland and New South Wales. Many families in these communities had traditionally used the local state or parish school for their children's primary education and had sent them to boarding school for their secondary schooling, or at least for years 11 and 12. However, the financial stresses caused by the recession put boarding school out of reach for many. This created added pressure for the existing local secondary schools to provide courses through to years 11 and 12.

Because of my experience in timetabling, I was often asked to travel to some of these remote towns, including Birdsville, Cunnamulla, Dalby, Chinchilla, Charleville, Quilpie, Thursday Island, Bourke, Brewarrina, Balranald, Nyngan and Broken Hill.

The demand for assistance in adapting to the changes made my life quite busy and challenging, not only in the formal educational settings, but in the social settings too. I was something of a city slicker and had much to learn about life in outback communities. The first time I visited Charleville, I booked into a local motel and decided to take a pre-dinner shower after my long drive. I could not get the hot water to work in the shower. A little frustrated, I went to the proprietor who was serving in the bar, chatting with a number of locals.

"Excuse me," I said, "I can't get any hot water from the shower in unit 12."

"Which tap are you using?"

"The hot tap."

I could tell by his amused eye contact with his mates that I was in trouble.

"We don't do that here. We use the cold tap for hot water and the hot tap for cold water."

I thought he was pulling my leg and I paused for a proper answer. I shook my head gently and waited.

"We're on bore water. The bore water is hot, so it goes into the normal pipes. If we want to cool it down, we do it with cold water from the hot water tank. Ain't that right fellas?"

Still trying to process his answer, I made a dignified retreat.

Another strong memory I have from my early visits to the outback involved a request to go to Quilpie to talk with people from the Catholic and State schools there. Quilpie is a small town about 200 kilometres west of Charleville. I was due in Quilpie on the Wednesday and decided to spend the previous night in the Charleville motel. I had a phone call in my room about 5.30 pm.

"That Mike Middleton?"

"Yes it is."

"You're coming to Quilpie tomorrow?"

"Yes I am."

"I'm Father Jeff Scully, parish priest from Quilpie. I don't want you visiting my school until I've talked with you. What time will you get here?"

"Between ten and eleven I reckon."

"OK, I'll meet you in the pub at 10.30. It's on the left as you come into town. See you then."

Next morning, I parked at the pub and went into the bar. Father Scully was waiting. He greeted me with a warm handshake and welcomed me to Quilpie. We chatted over coffee.

"You know if that Jesus fellow came to Earth today, he wouldn't go near the Vatican. He'd come here to Quilpie. This is the real world."

We chatted for half an hour. He was salt of the Earth. I learnt much about him, his school and his community. His parish school catered for day students as well as boarders from the surrounding areas, including from Aboriginal families. He died in 2015, an absolute icon of the outback.

Another strong memory involved a consultancy on Thursday Island. The week-long consultancy included a student-free-day to allow for a teachers' conference. During the conference the Director of Curriculum from Brisbane gave a late morning speech about the new Queensland curriculum that had been developed in Brisbane. At the end of his speech, there were some questions. Then the conference organiser announced that it was time for lunch and that grace would be led by Bishop Ted, an ageing Torres Strait Islander with snowy white hair. I was sitting next to the Curriculum Director as Bishop Ted rose to his feet.

"Lord, as we prepare for our meal, let us contemplate ways of freeing our curriculum from the city-based pattern. Let us have a curriculum that celebrates blue water, turtles, dolphins, coral and the smell of salt water. May our students love where they live and nurture this place and its community." (My paraphrased memory).

The Director's face was in his hands. I felt for him. The islanders had already designed a T-shirt to commemorate the conference.

I loved this strand of my work. I learnt so much about the life and cultures of different communities, particularly those in outback Queensland and New South Wales.

Chapter 9
Education at the Crossroads

Around the turn of the century, changing economic circumstances led to a different attitude to schooling and in particular to secondary schooling. There were discussions about the best ways of developing a curriculum suited to the times. Should it continue to be an aggregate of subjects, or should it be reshaped to reflect a new approach involving some variation on the 'new basics' or 'essential learnings'?

I am not an economist. However, it was clear to me that under the Hawke, Keating and Howard governments, economic imperatives were having a strong impact on the work of schools. There was a new focus on international trade, with a reduction in protective tariffs. There was also a parallel privatisation of many government services including telecommunications, banks, airports and Qantas. Between 1990 and 1997, the value of Australia's privatisation was 45 billion dollars, second only to the UK. (*Privatisation in Australia:* The Bulletin, December 1997). As a result, the federal government changed its priorities for schooling quite dramatically. Symbolically, the Commonwealth Schools Commission was discontinued in 1988 and its functions incorporated into the National Board of Employment, Education and Training (NBEET). This emphasised schooling as a process preparing and training people for jobs. In a speech given at Woodridge High School in Brisbane on 9th September 1986, Prime Minister Bob Hawke explained the aims of the Participation and Equity Project which his government had initiated in 1984.

"If Australians are to compete in the increasingly competitive international market, then the level of skill across the whole population must be increased. One way of making us increasingly competitive is for it to be the norm, rather than the exception, that young people complete a full secondary education, or its equivalent. The program's goals are ambitions. It aims to change the whole experience of school or college to create genuine opportunities for students who were previously excluded."

The new approach opened the way for secondary schools to be more flexible, allowing them to introduce 'work experience' and 'transition education'. In many communities, the links between schools and local industries were strengthened. There was a focus on retention into years 11 and 12, not just for aspiring university students, but for students headed towards careers in tourism, technology and trades. Home economics became 'catering and hospitality'. The changed ethos gave schools more room to innovate and there was a significant cultural shift in the way teachers and administrators viewed schooling.

Independently of these broad social and economic trends in Australia, the late 1980s and the 1990s saw two men from Harvard University, Howard Gardner and William Spady, stimulating a great deal of global discussion about teaching methods and curriculum structures. Howard Gardner is famous for his concept of multiple intelligences.[23] His work at the time suggested that humans exhibit at least seven identifiable and distinct kinds of intelligence. These included intelligences that could be described as:

- linguistic
- logical-mathematical
- spatial-visual
- musical
- kinaesthetic
- interpersonal
- intrapersonal.

Gardner's theory created a great deal of debate. More than anything, it challenged teachers to think about their students differently, realising the range of skills and talents that were sometimes overlooked in the formal classroom. While it was not Gardner's intention, his work also gave rise to the concept of 'learning styles' where teachers began to speak of 'visual learners', 'auditory learners', 'kinaesthetic learners' and the like.

Gardner had two specific involvements in Australian education. He was a consultant to the Australian Children's Television Foundation (ACTF) as it developed its series of children's programs titled Lift Off. The series was designed so that each of the animated characters epitomised one of the particular intelligences Gardner had identified. I was a Board Member of the ACTF at the time and appreciated Gardner's commitment and enthusiasm.

I was also involved with Howard Gardner while I was a guest speaker at the 1999 Annual Conference of the Australian Primary Principals' Association held in Hobart. I was interviewing him 'online' from his office at Harvard. The theme of the discussion was that recognised geniuses were often slow learners because they learnt thoroughly, taking time to explore concepts fully before moving on. There was a humorous twist to the interchange when he asked me to speak more slowly because of my accent. My cheeky reply was that I didn't have an accent; he did. He appreciated the quip. The audience did too.

William Spady was the second influential Harvard thinker. He developed the concept of Outcomes Based Education (OBE).[24] For a decade, his influence was strong, particularly in NSW and Queensland. Spady believed that education should equip learners to be active agents in creating a better world for themselves and their communities. He did not believe a curriculum that was an aggregate of traditional subject disciplines fitted the bill. Rather, he saw the need for citizens to be morally and ethically strong, capable of collaborative decision making, and skilled in the use of emerging technologies. He talked of backward mapping to achieve these outcomes for learners. He believed this mapping should be customised to meet local contexts, providing a variety of pathways and rates of learning.

Unfortunately, this concept of outcomes-based learning was too 'broad brush' and insufficiently defined. It was often interpreted selectively by educators to justify their own beliefs about education. The major problem was an attempt to marry an outcomes-based approach with a set of newly developed subject syllabuses labelled 'Key Learning Areas' (KLAs). The KLAs initially varied from state to state but included English, Mathematics, Science, Social Sciences, Arts, HPE (Health and Physical Education), Languages other than English, and Technology.

During the 1990s, teachers and curriculum writers in Queensland and NSW began to identify in detail the 'outcomes' for each of these KLAs at each year level. This was time consuming and frustrating work, both for those trying to document the outcomes and for those in the classroom trying to use them for planning and assessment. It was a situation far removed from Spady's initial well intentioned concept. He listed the kinds of superficialities that contaminated the integrity of his concept. He said that educators mistakenly tack outcomes onto pre-existing syllabuses instead of designing the syllabuses to achieve the defined outcomes. He also rejected the practice of tying desired outcomes directly to a yearly calendar.[25]

An initiative that paralleled Spady's work was the attempt in Australia (particularly in Queensland and Tasmania) to introduce a set of 'New Basics' into school curricula. The concept of 'new basics' had been raised by Brian Littleproud's Ministerial Curriculum Council in 1989. It was further developed by Professor Alan Luke, and James Ladwig as part of a team at the University of Queensland. The New Basics approach was trialled in a number of Queensland primary and secondary schools from the mid-1990s. It involved school communities identifying the kinds of knowledge and skills that the future would require and designing a curriculum accordingly. The aim was that students would engage in relevant projects culminating in 'rich tasks'. Despite some spectacular successes, the fundamental changes in pedagogy and the wording of achievements was a culture shock for many teachers and parents. In any case, as we shall see, the trials were discontinued in 2006 as national events flooded the agenda.

Tasmania interpreted the 'new basics' quite differently. Under Education Minister Paula Wriedt, it identified a set of 'essential learnings'. The proposed K–10 curriculum replaced subjects such as maths, science, English and history with a set of learning goals involving thinking, communicating, personal futures, social responsibility and world futures. There were many younger teachers who embraced the ideas enthusiastically. However, the community at large found the lack of old labels and the new terminology confusing. As was the case with the 'new basics', the essential learnings did not survive intact beyond 2006.

Chapter 10
A Melting Pot

The decades spanning the new millennium were rich with ideas and initiatives. Many were responses to the new priorities linking schooling with the economy. While some of the initiatives were quite radical, they accepted without question the essential paradigm framing Australian schooling. The curriculum was an aggregate of subjects and students moved through their schooling in yearly 'jumps'.

Within this paradigm, the demand for creative timetabling solutions was intense. Schools were challenged to create more flexible timetables allowing for 'work experience' and 'transition education'. The links between schools and local industries were strengthened. This changed ethos gave schools more room to innovate and there was a significant cultural shift in the way teachers and administrators viewed senior schooling. Some secondary schools were moving to a four-day week for years 11 and 12. Others were 'splitting' the school day so that the junior school and the senior school had different starting and finishing times. Many schools were adjusting their senior school programs to take account of students' engagement in part-time work.

In May 2007, I was asked by the Queensland Studies Authority to write a publication describing ways that secondary schools could implement the new Queensland syllabuses.[26] This was to be of particular interest to smaller country schools looking to provide a viable year 11 and 12 program for their students. Unskilled work had largely disappeared and

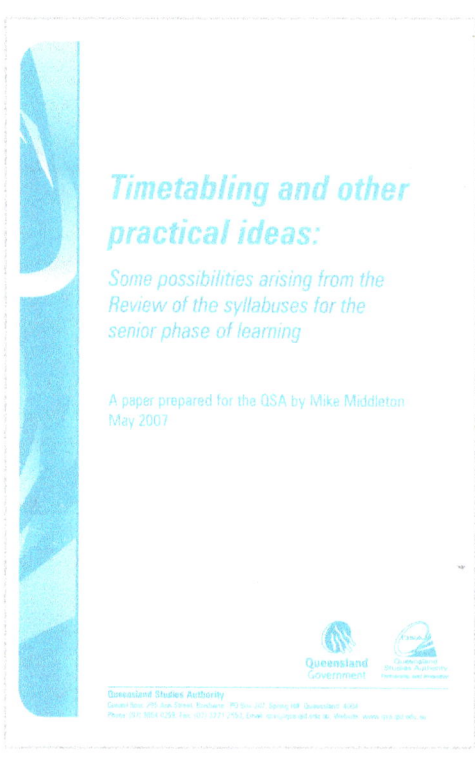

leaving after year 10 was not a good option. Because of my experience in timetabling, I was able to suggest a number of strategies schools could use. I drew attention to the kinds of initiatives schools around Australia were taking as well as those I had developed myself.

I described the structured learning centres that many schools had used to provide extra opportunities for students. Scores of schools had used this approach. They utilised a space close to the library for small groups of students to pursue courses that would otherwise have been impossible. Sometimes, these extra courses were online. I remember visiting St John's Catholic School in Roma where students were studying four languages, using online resources and guided by a learning mentor. The centres also enabled students to work around the 'line clashes' all schools suffer, where two subjects offered at the same time (on the same choice line) were chosen by some students. The centre gave them the opportunity to study both subjects.

In smaller schools, it was often better to offer low candidature senior subjects every second year at twice the time intensity. This doubled the viability of many subjects.

Large as well as small schools had used 'line days' to provide extra opportunities. This meant that, say, once a term, each subject that students studied would be provided with a whole day. In this way, events like excursions and learning experiences requiring extended time periods could be facilitated. Some schools used a four-day week in their senior school. Others had devised different ways of providing for part-time and re-entry students.

Partly because of this work with the Queensland Studies Authority, I found myself in demand in Western Australia. Schools there were seeking ways of structuring and timetabling middle schooling alongside their primary and secondary schools. Consequently, I worked extensively in many Perth schools including Wesley College, Aquinas, Santa Maria, Presbyterian Ladies College, Scotch College and Perth College.

However, despite these activities, perhaps because of them, I was questioning the regulated organisational framework of schooling in Australia. The challenges around the turn of the century brought many of the issues into stark focus. When I talked with teachers about timetabling, many rolled their eyes and responded that this issue was one for administrators, not for classroom teachers. For them, teaching issues weren't about administration. They were about what happens in classrooms. Teaching is about the curriculum, assessment and pedagogy. 'Timetabling' is for administrators.

I realised that there were two quite distinct dimensions of thinking about the management of time. Most teachers saw 'timetabling' decisions as deciding when different subjects are taught, or what time the school day should start and finish, or how much student-free time a teacher should have each week. They were micro-managed administrative decisions made within a set of historical 'givens'. With a few significant exceptions, the givens had been unquestioned aspects of Australian schooling for generations. The curricular pattern in almost all schools in the Australian states at the time could be represented by the following schema.

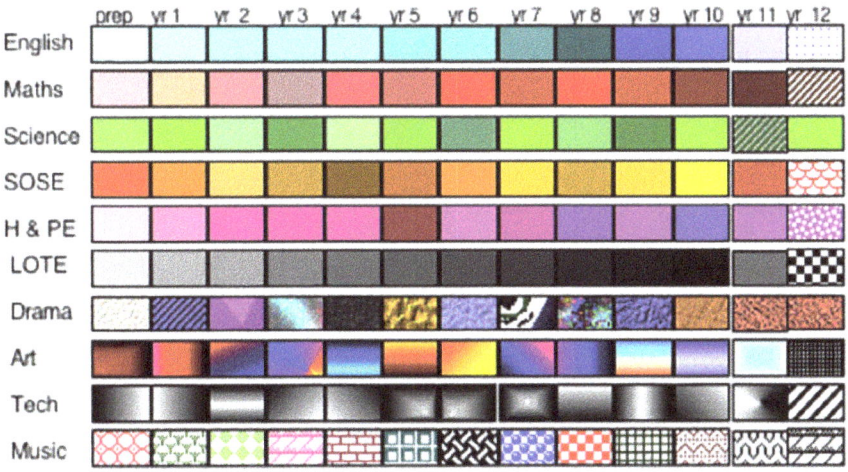

The schema had two dimensions. The 'horizontal' dimension involved the lock-step progression of students through their years of schooling. All students needed seven years of primary school education and at least four years of secondary schooling. Students should progress through schooling in steps based on the Earth years. In this way, students could be compared with each other and graded accordingly. Socially, it was best and natural for young people to learn with similar aged peers.

The vertical dimension involved the organisation of the curriculum. The curriculum is an aggregate of 'subjects'. Different subjects are taught at different times, and in secondary schools, by different teachers. The school day is divided into 'periods' or 'sessions' so that different subjects can be taught.

In essence, this curriculum pattern involved about 120 'compartments'. Each had its own programming and its own assessment. Each started at the beginning of a year, and finished at the end. During their schooling, students were typically 'delivered' nearly all of these hundred plus curriculum elements.

The givens implicit in this kind of schema were being challenged because they had a profound, limiting and sometimes destructive effect on curriculum design, on assessment and reporting, on pedagogy and on school cultures. I was among a number of educators seeking alternative approaches.

Chapter 11
Continuous Learning

A major passion of mine was to continue challenging the 'horizontal' dimension by seeking ways of implementing a more continuous, developmental approach to learning. I'd already spent much time and effort on this in secondary schooling with the development of vertical timetabling. I wanted to explore the concept in primary schooling. There was an optimistic belief among some primary school people that it was possible to treat students as individual learners and allow them to progress at their own rate. This was especially true in small schools of one, two or three teachers. It was also true in the Steiner context where teachers often worked with the same cohort of students across several years. However, this ideal situation was very rarely achieved in larger schools outside these contexts because students were organised in 'batches' and moved through the school system on a yearly basis from one teacher to the next as if on an assembly line.

This lockstep 'industrial approach' has required a particular age to be the starting point for the assembly line. Historically, the pattern has varied from state to state. Consider the date Tasmania has used. Students have had to be five years of age on the first of January to start their schooling. While the following hypothetical example is extreme, it illustrates the situation for many thousands of Australian children working within time-bound patterns.

Toby and Tom are twins. Toby was born late on the night of 31st December, Tom in the early morning of 1st January. Accordingly, Toby begins his schooling in the year 2001, Tom in 2002. Toby enters secondary schooling in 2008, Tom in 2009, irrespective of their relative rates of learning. Why should a student born in January be permanently a year behind one born in December? It is an administrative convenience, but an educational absurdity.

Outside the school systems, learning is often much less time-dependent. The scouting movement has long organised its learning in a continuous pathway from Tenderfoot to Second Class to First Class to Queen. Students who learn a musical instrument take the time they need to proceed to the more advanced levels. Universities allow students to take up to nine years to complete a degree others finish in three years

I found the following graphic useful in explaining time as a resource to teachers, parents and students. The speed with which a large group of people learns anything is normally distributed. I.Q. exemplifies this.

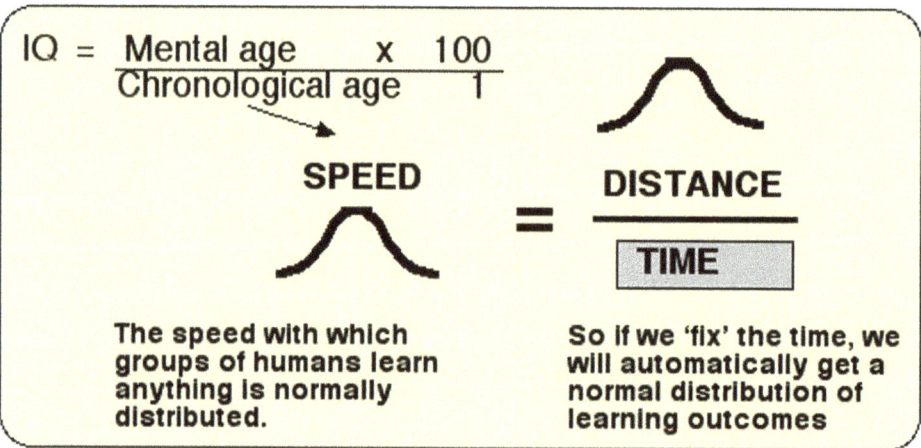

Within this time-fixed, lock-stepped paradigm, there has been a variety of ways classes have been arranged in schools. In about a sixth of government schools and in most non-government schools, the classes are divided into straight year groups. These are clearly lock-stepped and often considered to be desirably 'neat'. However, the great majority of government schools, and some non-government country schools, have to arrange a pattern of 'composite' classes, because the numbers do not allow 'straight' classes. These composite patterns are also fundamentally 'lock-stepped', and often criticised as less than ideal because teachers are coping with more than one 'year group' at once.

During the 1980s and 1990s, there was a vibrant 'Multi-age Association', particularly strong in Queensland. The belief was that multi-age groupings avoided the tendency to treat students *en masse* and encouraged teachers to take account of their individual learning needs. In the 1990s, the New South Wales Curriculum Directorate described an alternative pattern it called a stage-based approach. Classes were organised around the stages of expected skill attainment. Stage 1 classes were kindergarten, year 1 and year 2. Stage 2 classes were years 3 and 4. Stage 3 classes were years 5 and 6. The aim was to provide some of the benefits and flexibility inherent in multi-age approaches. This NSW strategy extended the unit of time to two or three years. However, it was still fundamentally lock-stepped (lock-lock/step-step).

The potential for continuity by breaking the time straitjacket is obvious in a small, one-teacher school. Imagine a school of 21 students, 2, 3 or 4 in each age group. The teacher will almost certainly teach according to the students' learning needs rather than their ages. Most students will complete their primary schooling in seven years. However, a few might need eight years and some might complete their schooling in six years. If this seems radical, bear in mind that a student taking eight years may be just a week older on graduation than another taking seven years. A graduating student taking six years might be only a week younger than one taking seven years.

To challenge the lockstep that does more than pay lip service to continuous learning in larger primary schools, there is a need to consider an alternative organisational approach.

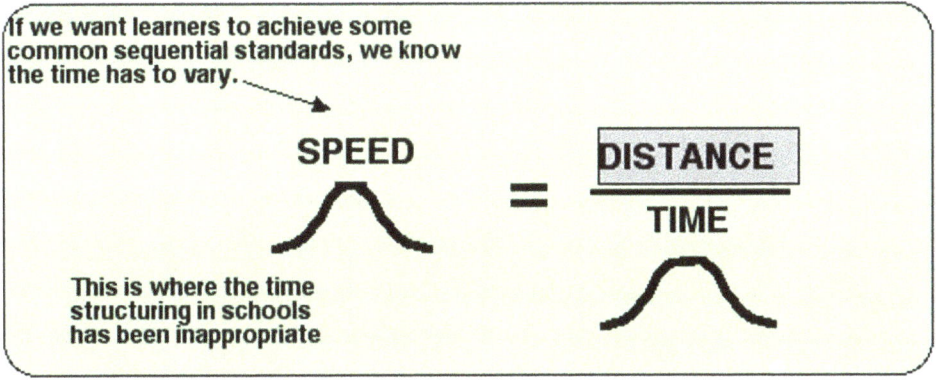

There is some learning that is fundamental and foundational. Different students will take different periods of time to achieve this learning. Children who have had little experience of the English language, or little engagement in reading or discussion at home, will take longer to achieve the necessary prerequisites. This does not mean they are permanently slower learners, or less intelligent. But the lock-step organisation keeps them permanently behind.

During the 1980s and 1990s, prior to the Australian Curriculum, I supported many primary schools in Queensland and New South Wales that did not have this limitation. These schools included Catholic schools like St Thomas' in Mareeba, and St Thomas More's in Toowoomba, Government schools like Walkerston Primary School near Mackay, Avoca Primary School in Gladstone and Merimbula State School in NSW as well as Lutheran schools like Bethany in Ipswich and Grace in Redcliffe. These stage-based schools had classes patterned in a way that facilitated true continuous learning. They divided the curriculum, and the groupings, into three overlapping 'stages'. Chapter 19 outlines the very simple way this can be done. For the moment though, we'll focus on the overall pattern.

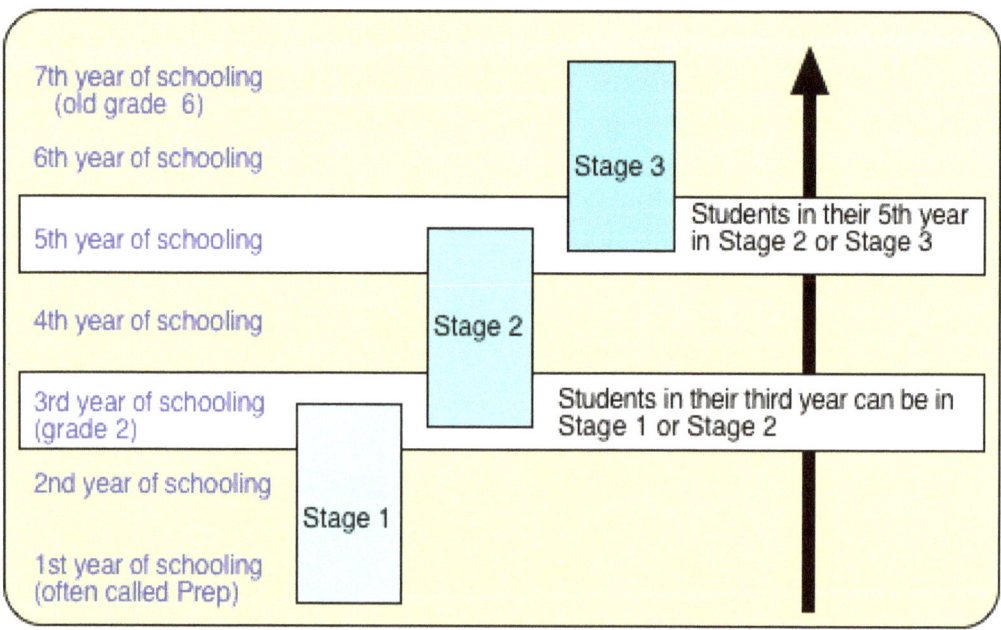

This pattern means that students can spend either two or three years in each stage. Most students follow a pattern like one of the following, completing the journey in seven years.

3 + 2 + 2   or 2 + 3 + 2   or 2 + 2 + 3.

For many students, it does not matter which of these three patterns applies. This provides the schools with a high degree of flexibility in their grouping, taking into account gender balance, friendship patterns and the like. A minority follows a 2 + 2 + 2 pattern, or a 3 + 3 + 2 pattern, depending on need.

Let's look at what a true stage-based approach means for individual students. We'll use five students as examples, looking first at their overall learning patterns and then how the details for each might best be handled.

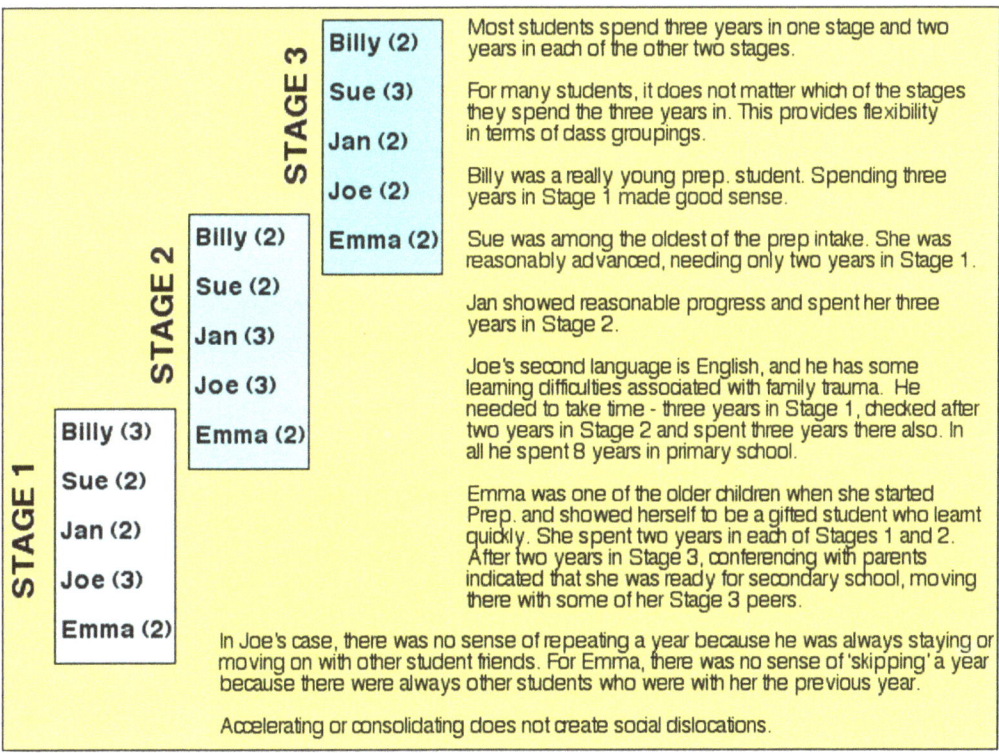

The vital difference between this pattern and the NSW 'stages' was the overlap. Late stage 1 was equivalent to early stage 2. Late stage 2 was equivalent to early stage 3. If this didn't happen, a 'stage-based' curriculum had little advantage over a year-based curriculum because students were still burdened with a time-locked learning program. Continuity implies that the 'rate' of learning is different for different students in different subjects and may vary from year to year with individual students.

The pattern these schools used provided individual students with the time they needed to complete primary school. Children from disadvantaged backgrounds could spend three years in stage 1 while some of their peers spent only two. This did not mean they were permanently behind because they would likely spend just two years in each of stages 2 and 3. Even if they needed eight years, there was nothing to lose. The resourcing of disadvantage has always been seen as more money. More TIME is what many need. The cost of the extra time is balanced by the savings among students who need only six years. A bonus for administrators and teachers is that the pattern creates the opportunity to equalise class sizes across the school and to have much more homogeneous classes without the disadvantages of 'streaming'.

The schools typically organised a literacy block and a numeracy block each day. Students were grouped into 'journey groups' for these blocks. The groups were called 'early', 'middle' and 'late' groups in each stage. Individual students progressed through these groups taking two or three years in each stage. Normally, the groupings remained spatially within the rooms used by home classes in the 'stage'. There was not a wholesale movement across the school (as sometimes happens in secondary schools).

It is important here to stress the difference between 'journey grouping' and 'streaming'. Every journey group has a mix of IQs (and by implication a mix of social backgrounds). All students are on a similar journey, not two or three different journeys.

During the1960s, 1970s and 1980s, there was a very strong push against 'streaming', both between schools and within schools. The critique came mainly from the 'left' side of politics, led by Jean Blackburn, Joan Kirner, Dean Ashenden and others. They rightly saw streaming students into 'ability groups' as elitist, and socio-economically biased. However, their critique *took for granted the year-based automatic progression of students*. The following illustrates the validity of their position.

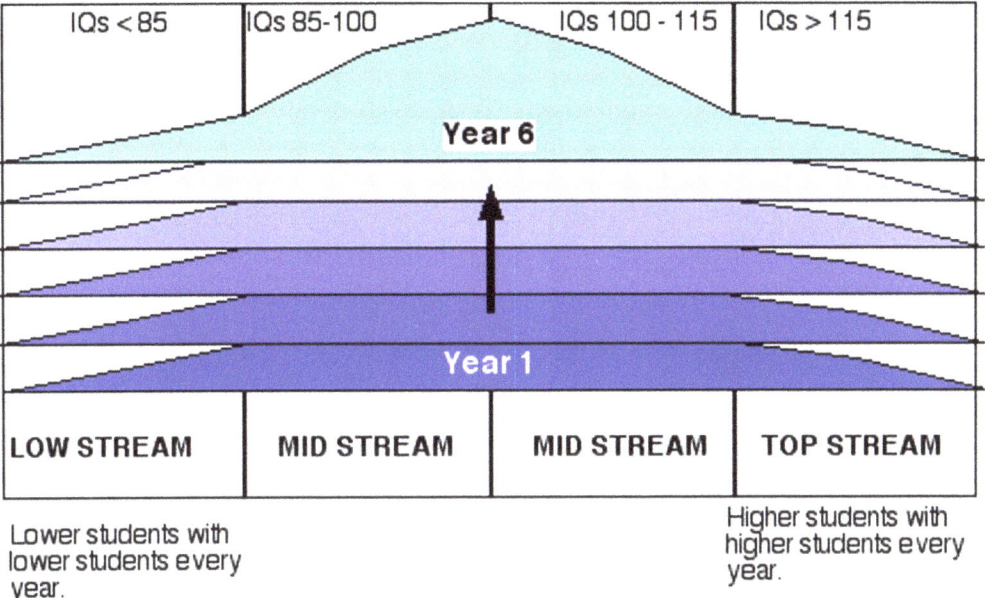

Using IQs as a label, it is easy to see that low IQ students, or students with disadvantaged backgrounds, will always be in groups with other similar students. And high-performing students will always be with other high-performing students. The divisiveness and the socio-economic implications of these practices are obvious. This is why, in most states, tripartite systems gave way to comprehensive systems. 'Streaming' was frowned upon and largely discontinued. **However, streaming was only ever needed because of year grouping. This has to be made clear within the profession and among policy makers.**

Once schools move away from a time-locked progression, students with similar learning needs can be grouped together without the negative effects that were involved in 'streaming'. This has huge implications for pedagogy, for the working conditions of teachers and for students whose pre-school years were devoid of much home support. The ability of these students to take three years in stage 1 gives many the time they need to achieve well, and to come into line with their age peers.

The stage-based schools used a two-year cycle right across the stages in subjects like science, the social sciences and the arts. This meant that there was continuity of learning in these areas no matter what the pattern of progress was for individual students.

In the early 2000s, many Queensland schools explored the most appropriate curriculum patterns for their teachers, students and communities. They were encouraged to share their experiences, including successes and failures, with other schools so that the 'system' as a whole could make progress. For example, in the Toowoomba Catholic Diocese, under its visionary Director Dr Bill Sultmann, the many Catholic primary schools were asked to nominate one of four curriculum patterns.

	Year based groupings	Stage based groupings
Aggregated Curriculum	OPTION A eg Sacred Heart	OPTION B eg St Anthony's
Integrated curriculum (warp/weft)	OPTION C eg St Columba's Dalby	OPTION D eg St Thomas More

There were regular meetings between representative staff of these schools so the pros and cons of each pattern could be determined. I worked in all these schools. The vibrancy among staff was obvious. A similar situation occurred in the Cairns Diocese. I remember tracking a particular group of initially disengaged students in a school in Mareeba. Prior to the school's implementation of a stage-based approach, these students were inactive in class, afraid to contribute for fear of being 'wrong'. Once they were in a group of peers working at their level, they couldn't wait to get involved. The transformation was spectacular, both in terms of their enjoyment of school and their learning progress.

Chapter 12

New Basics or Subjects?

Like others, I was also concerned about the subject-based curriculum pattern. From the very beginning of my teaching career, I had been at pains to make sure the science I was teaching was embedded in a broad context involving wonder, logic, language, human history, ethical questions and the future of humanity on the planet. I found that these connections provided real relevance for my students. The late 1990s saw debates among educators that amounted to an either/or solution to curriculum planning. This was frustrating. It implied that *either* we continue to use traditional subject disciplines as the framework for our teaching *or* we redefine the curriculum framework around a set of 'new basics' or 'essential learnings'.

I knew that it was unrealistic to believe the three-thousand-year history of subject disciplines could be completely discarded. It had stood the test of time and was inextricably linked to the way adult society viewed schooling. Discarding the 'subjects' altogether would never be politically acceptable. However, the disciplines were often treated as 'silos', as separate fields of knowledge. This was particularly true in secondary schools where teachers were specialised. Not only were the subject disciplines taught in 'silos', there was also a pecking order among them. I remember with deep regret my early years of teaching in comprehensive schools where, on 'speech night', the teachers of English, maths, science and the humanities wore academic gowns while those who taught the other subjects wore 'civvies'. The academic subjects were called the 'core' subjects. They were the compulsory ones. Why?

After all, those who grew food, cooked food, built houses, built roads, mined metals, wired houses for electricity, cleaned buildings, made clothes and collected waste were essential for human survival. Why were they less important than algebra or Shakespeare? For me, the answer was disturbing. It homed right in on the real purpose of schooling. The reason why the academic subjects were important was that they were measurable, cheaply and on paper, and were capable of providing a comparative score. In this way, school leavers could be allocated into the 'appropriate' layers of the workforce and the society. It was not a core curriculum. It was a (s)core curriculum. I remember asking my daughter Ariane what she thought of the maths she was learning in year 9 at high school.

"Maths is just for finding out how smart you are," was her response. "We won't ever use most of it."

In terms of employment and job satisfaction, the traditional pecking order is problematic anyway. For example, the 2018 Graduate Outcomes Survey showed 97.7% of Australians with a Certificate III in Carpentry gained a job. However, only 73% of university graduates were employed within four months of graduation and only about half of these felt their education qualification was relevant to their work.

How could the hierarchical silo effect be overcome? The subject-based educators of academia were particularly sceptical about any variation to a curriculum that did not involve the 'disciplines' as separate and unique studies. There was much debate about integration and how it destroyed or diluted the rigorous integrity of the disciplines. Many saw 'integration' as a populist, Mickey Mouse approach that replaced real rigour and intellect with an attempt to sugar-coat the disciplines to make them less daunting. My suspicion was that many of the people who were creating the syllabuses were so narrowly specialised that they were uncomfortable finding links with other disciplines anyway.

I came to the conclusion that the subject disciplines and the 'new basics' were not incompatible. Indeed, the disciplines could be seen as the vehicles by which the new basics could be achieved. The new basics could be a means of highlighting the uniqueness and rigour of the disciplines. The two 'options' were mutually supportive. I invented a weaving metaphor to illustrate the concept. The new basics could be the warp in a piece of weaving.

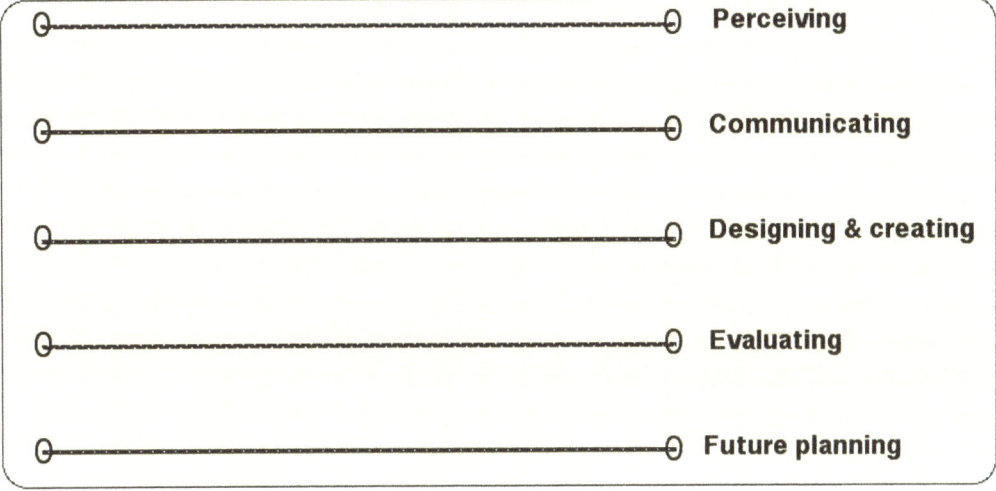

The cross threads, the weft, could be represented by the unique disciplines.

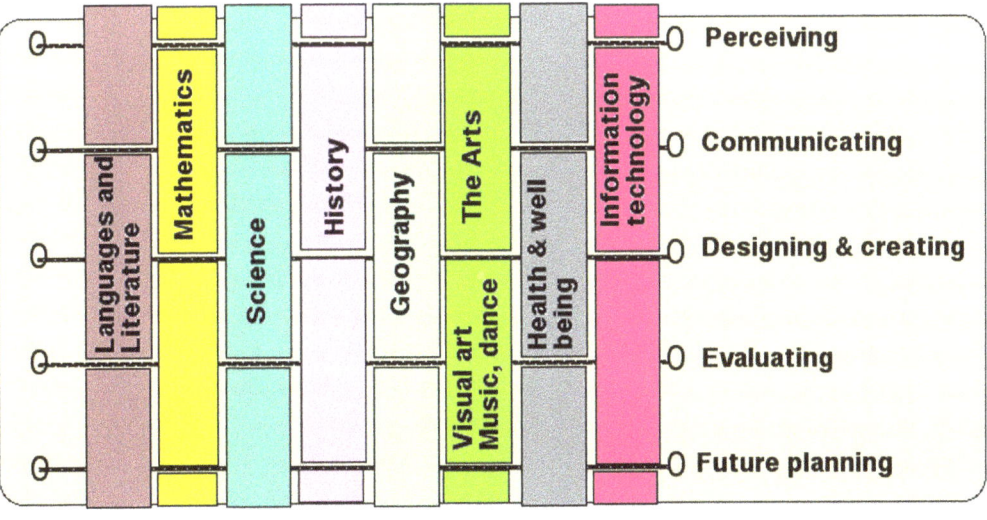

How does a scientist perceive the world and communicate the perception? How is this different from the way a poet might see the world, or a mathematician, a geographer, an artist or a musician? Each discipline has a unique way of seeing the world. Each designs and creates in its own way. And each makes its own contribution to the way we analyse the world we live in and the way we plan ahead. The role of languages, science, mathematics, history, recreation and geography in deciding how a society responds to a pandemic or to climate change is a good example of the need to see both the uniqueness and inter-relatedness among the disciplines. I published this concept in one of the MCCC's discussion papers.

This kind of curriculum fabric would require those writing subject syllabuses, at whatever level, to use a common framework represented by the 'new basics'. I do not believe this approach would restrict the syllabus writers in terms of the integrity of the disciplines. It would certainly free up teachers to consider a range of approaches to curriculum planning, pedagogy and assessment. The 'new' basics are not really new at all. They have always been there. What is important is the need to have a curriculum that 'hangs together', that makes existential sense to learners who need to understand the richness of the human experience and who need to see education as more than a competition for places in a layered society.

PART 2

Chapter 13
Politics Intervenes

Ironically, while the 1970s Whitlam government's policies in schooling were designed to support diversity and change within devolved systems, its foray into schooling created the opportunity for later national governments to become involved quite differently and create an opposite effect. In 1996, when John Howard became Prime Minister, the issue of curriculum development became political.

As we have seen, state teachers' federations had joined the ACTU in 1984. Despite teachers being broadly representative of Australian society, this unionisation spooked some conservative politicians. Addressing the South Australian State Council of the Liberal Party in Adelaide on 21st August, 2004, John Howard stated that teacher unions pursued ideology, political correctness and class envy rather than the interests of ordinary Australians and their children. Nevertheless, Howard's early Ministers for Education were opposed to any idea of a national curriculum. David Kemp believed it would be impossible to obtain state government agreement on a high quality national curriculum and in any case, it would be a mistake to replace a state monopoly curriculum with a national monopoly curriculum. The following Minister, Brendan Nelson, was against a common curriculum. "I'm actually opposed to the idea of a national curriculum throughout schooling." He referred to it as a prescription for mediocrity.[27]

In 2006, Julie Bishop became Federal Education Minister. It is worth noting that, at the time, every Australian state and territory had a Labor government – Premiers Beattie (Q), Iemma (NSW), Bracks (Vic), Lennon (Tas), Rann (SA), Gallop (WA), Martin (NT) and Stanhope (ACT). In that year, Julie Bishop told the History Teachers' Association (6th October), "We need to take school curriculum out of the hands of ideologues in the State and Territory education bureaucracies and give it to, say, a national board of studies."[28]

This recommendation was not couched in political terms. However, some of her colleagues were not convinced. John Roskam, a prominent Liberal Party member and adviser to David Kemp (and later the Executive Director of the Institute of Public Affairs) wrote (*The Age* 11th October 2006), "The Minister should be supported in her desire to improve the quality of education and she has raised some valid issues. However, her proposed solution – a national curriculum – is completely the wrong way to fix the problem. Giving control to a single authority, in this case the Commonwealth Department of Education, over what's studied by Australia's 3 million school students is a disaster waiting to happen …"

Nevertheless, a national curriculum was legislated and introduced from 2009. Teams of specialist curriculum writers in more than eight subject areas set about creating syllabuses that were aggregated into a national curriculum, based on year levels. Ironically, some 'cross curriculum' elements were added, creating yet more courses to aggregate.

Three justifications were raised by Bishop and her supporters in proposing the Australian Curriculum. The first involved the fact that service men and women, among others, were being transferred across states. Their children would be disadvantaged if the curriculum wasn't standardised. Yet over twenty-five thousand international students from ten Asian countries were enrolled in Australian schools in 2019 and most performed well, on average better than Australian students.

A second justification was the need to develop learning programs suited to the 21st century. Unfortunately, a nationally centralised model of curriculum development is unable effectively to respond to one of the main features of 21st century life, that of change. Recent history shows that it takes several years for a new national syllabus to be developed and trialled. The phasing in over the school years may take another four or five years at least. This means that Australian secondary students are studying a curriculum at least a decade old. For some elements of the curriculum, this doesn't matter. Shakespeare and Pythagoras are timeless.

Global and local events aren't. Students' parents are talking about such matters as Covid-19, bushfires, floods, Islamophobia, immigration, global warming (or not) and US Presidents' policies and behaviours. They live in a real-time world where media coverage is instant, and sometimes unreliable, where space probes are launched regularly, and where countries are developing alternative ways of powering trains, cars and electricity networks. Almost daily, there are additions to the applications available on the devices children use, sophisticated applications that leave most parents and teachers behind. For many students, school is becoming marginalised. It does not relate to the challenges and fears and hopes they are grappling with. Many disengage.

A third Bishop argument, and one that is referred to in the introductory statement to the Australian Curriculum, involves economies of scale. It assumes that one curriculum development group can effectively do it for all. It sees the curriculum as a package that can be delivered *en masse* to three million students across the nation.

This is in complete contradiction to the advice of educators like Garth Boomer, Malcolm Skilbeck, Peter Karmel and Bill Connell over the previous half century. In their view, people in all walks of life and all corners of the continent needed to be involved in curriculum making. Internalising, interpreting and analysing our history and likely futures so that we can best share insights, knowledge and skills with the next generation ought to be a nationwide activity, part of a healthy nation's deep culture, as once it was.

By surrendering our formal curriculum making to a central authority, we sterilise that culture. Arguing that centralised curriculum development creates economies of scale by avoiding duplication is as mad as saying that we ought to centralise music-making so that one orchestra takes it on for the nation. Curriculum development is an essential element of learning at every level, from the nation, to states, to schools and, as we have seen, to individual learners and even to pre-schoolers. When we withdraw curriculum-making to a central place, we cripple creativity, our national and individual resilience and our adaptability.

However, if one takes into account John Howard's sentiments and Julie Bishop's words to the History Teachers' Association, the real reason for the National Curriculum was to take what is taught in schools out of the hands of teachers. American educator Richard Curwin comments on this approach. "So what do we make of programs that claim to be 'teacher proof?' The growing trend to incorporate programs that are devoid of teachers deciding what to teach, when to teach it and how to teach it, is a disgrace not only to teachers but to all educators, and even to children. Not only do students suffer from scripted programs, teachers suffer, too. Teachers lose their creativity, their enthusiasm and their love of teaching. They lose their desire to be teachers. Many quit."[29]

Complicating matters for Australian teachers was the introduction of NAPLAN. This was also conceived by Julie Bishop as Education Minister in the Howard Government. It was developed in 2007 by the Australian Curriculum, Reporting and Assessment Authority (ACARA) but because the government changed in December 2007, it was first administered in 2008 under the Rudd Government. This was the first time that students across the country were assessed using common test instruments. Since then, students in years 3, 5, 7 and 9 have undertaken the tests every year.

Chapter 14
Effects of a Central Curriculum

Over the past six decades, I have worked by school or system invitation in over four hundred Australian schools in all states and territories. Since 2009, most of my work has been in Queensland and Western Australia, with a smattering in Victoria and Tasmania. The culture of schools has shifted quite noticeably during this time. Instead of teachers discussing what they could do to meet student needs, take up opportunities or overcome difficulties, the dominant attitude has become one of questioning what is allowed to be done.

ACARA's hope was that the Australian Curriculum could be used flexibly by schools to develop programs that met the needs of their particular students. It was also hoped that schools would implement the Australian Curriculum in ways that valued teachers' professional knowledge, reflected local contexts and took into account the backgrounds of individual families and communities. The flexibility was good in theory. However, the aspiration does not take account of the dynamics of bureaucracies, especially disparate bureaucracies. At what level within a layered 'system' can the flexibility be exercised – state level? Independent School Authority? Regional? School? Teaching team? Individual teachers? Students?

We are dealing here with a dysfunctional arrangement. Normally, a layered bureaucratic structure enables initiatives and directives to be dissipated 'down' through the layers. However, if the curriculum is to meet local needs, and the unique needs of individual young people, the initiative has to be at the 'bottom' and the 'permission seeking' has to flow upwards. How does accountability operate in this situation?

In my observation and judgement, flexibility is often stymied by someone, or some group in the 'chain of command' either uncertain of their degree of freedom or intent on asserting their 'leadership', believing it to be their professional responsibility. Leaders at a level in a bureaucracy are used to being 'in charge' of those below them. Responding to requests from below for modifications to the curriculum are sometimes perceived to be at odds with their top-down leadership status. They hesitate to say 'yes' when they are unsure whether their own line manager would approve. This is understandable because the state and regional curriculum branches have largely been disbanded. How do school leaders know what is acceptable and what is not? The syllabuses being written in year-based detail does not help. Passing any request for significant change all the way up the line is a logistical impossibility.

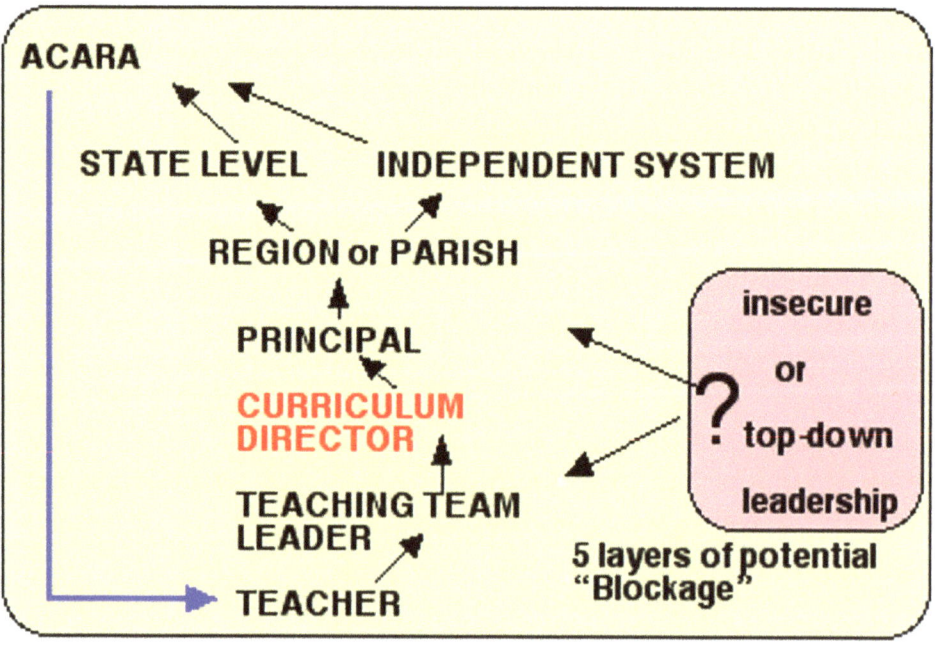

The dilemma is highlighted by the recent review of the NSW curriculum.[36] This amounts to intervention at the state level to 'flex' the Australian Curriculum.

Emerging difficulties in curriculum management have become obvious to me during my later consultancies. Suggestions of stage-based options in primary schools were met with

"We cannot do that now. The curriculum is in years. Anyway, what about NAPLAN? It is in years too."

A number of events stand out in my memory. I was observing a science lesson in a year 10 class in Townsville, Queensland. The teacher introduced the lesson with the words,

"What we have to do next is…" I found this disturbing because it highlighted the fact that the teacher was under external constraint. It was at odds with any hint of a negotiated curriculum, or even a curriculum that the teacher had planned himself. I reflected on the changed accountability and culture that seems to have occurred in many classrooms. During my own years of teaching, I always felt accountable to my students and their families. Unhappy, disengaged or underperforming students stimulated me to adjust the curriculum, and my teaching, to bring them back into the fold.

Now there is accountability in two directions. Teachers feel they are under scrutiny to make sure they are adhering to the demands of a national curriculum. So often I have heard them express frustration because the two accountabilities are at odds.

"If I teach what they're telling me to teach, my kids aren't going to engage."

In my discussions with teachers in both primary and secondary schools, it became clear that this ambivalence in accountability dramatically diminishes the effectiveness of teaching. I heard comments like,

"There is so much assessment and paperwork, I don't have time to prepare lessons anymore." (secondary humanities teacher in Queensland).

"I don't have time to fart. There's no way I have time to prepare quality lessons the way I used to. I pay to subscribe to Teach-starter or Twinkle so that my lessons just roll off the net. I flick pass them to the kids. Our collaborative meetings are not about planning. They're about ensuring accountability. It sucks." (primary school teacher in Tasmania).

"The majority of the 18 classes in my school have part-time or contract teachers because if you teach full time, you don't have a life." (primary school teacher). Research indicates that, Australia-wide, 82% of primary school teachers are female. By 2015, 31% of them were part-time.[30]

"I reckon only about ten per cent of my professional time is spent engaged in effective face to face teaching." (primary school teacher).

This estimate is not unreasonable given that "on average, teachers spend about 52.8 hours per week on school-related activities."[31] Ten percent represents about an hour per working day. In one primary school I visited, there were five teachers of parallel, composite year 3/4 classes. They were told that if one of them was away, there would be no need for a relief teacher. The classes could be collapsed into four classes because, in the words of the principal, 'You should all be doing the same thing anyway.'

The following quote from Merryn McKinnon is one that I now identify with, yet one that was not true for most of my life as an educator.

"We want to create a nation of critical thinking, creative, flexible and innovative people who understand the importance of collaboration. Yet teachers are not supported to be truly innovative and the system is far from flexible, creating barriers to desired practice and frustration. Failing to recognise this will ensure we continue to lose the teachers we need most."[32]

Since I began writing this book, my daughter Sarah has resigned from primary school teaching two years into the job. After completing a PhD in law and lecturing at the tertiary level for some years, she was absolutely frustrated with primary school teaching. She found a very small percentage of her time and energy actually involved teaching. Meetings, 'paperwork' and 'assessment' dominated her attention. Her creative instincts were continually inhibited by the need to adhere to a 'lowest common denominator' attitude that pervaded the teaching culture.

In my view, the teaching culture in Australia will take decades to recover. The Australian Curriculum, and to a lesser extent NAPLAN, have altered the culture of the teaching service in two important ways. The first involves the quantitative load on teachers. The second, much more damaging effect, involves the way teachers view their work, and the way potential teachers view it.

Primary school teachers are in a perfect logistic storm. At every year level, they are expected to teach all subjects in year-defined steps, despite the fact that the 'learning age' of students in their classes often spans six years. (For example, by year 6 the reading age spread is typically about seven years). The automatic yearly progression of 'classes' forces some students on before they are ready and holds others back. Both these groups are in danger of disengagement. It is not surprising then that the Australian PISA (Program for International Student Assessment) results show that the percentage of 'under-achieving' students is increasing, and the percentage of 'over-achieving' students is declining. Some teachers are very skilled in meeting the needs of all students in their classes, but the time and energy required is stressful and time-consuming. For many, the time pressure makes it necessary to teach to the 'middle' of the range. As a result, students at either end disengage and create extra behavioural issues.

Making matters worse, the 'mass processing' can easily become mere tokenism in subjects like history, geography, science, languages and the arts because the 'basics' of literacy and numeracy measured by NAPLAN dominate the agenda. Finding time for the rest is difficult and sometimes impossible. As standards have fallen, the political reflex is to demand accountability from teachers. The time and effort teachers need to undertake the resulting paperwork erodes standards even further because there is less time for real teaching.

The introduction of NAPLAN and of the Australian Curriculum have coincided with what many see as a crisis in teaching. Whether or not these introductions caused the crisis needs to be addressed. The following news release reflects much of what I have heard during my consulting and is typical of many messages Australians have been getting.

Australian teachers are 'at the end of their tethers' and abandoning the profession, sparking a crisis

Difficult kids, abusive parents, endless admin and less actual teaching. No wonder almost half of new Aussie teachers quit within five years.

 Shannon Molloy 27 comments   news.com.au JANUARY 13, 2019 8:25PM

The release goes on to say that "Australia is facing an education crisis as hordes of disillusioned and burnt-out teachers flee the profession, with potentially damaging ramifications for the whole country. Former educators have spoken to news.com.au about the "miserable" conditions driving an estimated 40 per cent of graduates to quit within the first five years of entering the workforce."

The abandoning of our profession is not limited to beginning teachers. Veterans are pulling the plug too. The news release quoted one such ex-teacher who described her experience.

"I went from being able to spend most of my time dedicated to my students, planning great lessons and putting my energy into my classroom, to being taken over by meetings, paperwork and checking boxes for the sake of it."

The crisis is made worse by the rapid decline in young people aspiring to be teachers. By 2018, there were ominous signs. On April 16th 2018, the ABC's "The Conversation" reported a number of troubling trends. The percentage of graduating students making teaching their first preference on entering university courses was dropping rapidly. For example, the University of Queensland saw a 44 per cent drop compared with the previous year. The Victorian Tertiary Admissions Centre had noted a forty per cent drop in 2017 compared with 2016. The Australian Catholic University reported a twenty per cent drop for its campuses in Queensland, New South Wales and Victoria.

These declines are clearly not related to the salaries of teachers. There was no sudden change in the trajectory of salaries. The decline results from a changed perception of teaching in Australia, both within the profession and without. By 2017, school leavers had experienced five or six years of their own schooling under the new, centralised regime. Their view of teaching was tainted accordingly.

Many of the best teachers I have worked with were passionate about the arts, about Australia's cultural life, about its literature and about the creative and human aspects of life on the planet. However, in 2020, the economic imperatives for Australian education seem to have gone too far for a nation that values the arts and cultural life. The relative costs of university courses for 2021 were manipulated to discourage students from choosing degrees seen to be economically irrelevant. Fees for humanities and communications subjects were lifted by 113 per cent. On the other hand, agriculture and maths degrees were planned to become 59 per cent cheaper while degrees in teaching, nursing, and clinical psychology were up to 42 per cent cheaper. Science, health, architecture, environmental science, IT and engineering degrees will be up to 18 per cent cheaper. It is yet to be seen whether the manipulation is able to convince more young people to take up teaching.

PART 3

Chapter 15

The Gonski Reports

There have been three major curriculum-related reports written since the Australian Curriculum was introduced.

In 2011, a committee chaired by David Gonski released a report commonly called the Gonski 1 Report.[33] It focused on inequality and the funding arrangements needed to address the issue. The Report drew attention to a significant and growing gap between the highest and lowest performing students, a gap disturbingly reflective of socio-economic status. Unsurprisingly, the gap between private schools and public schools was quite dramatic. The review reiterated the findings of the OECD that poorly educated people hamper the development of a resilient economy. They damage social cohesion and require greater spending on public health, on social support and on combatting criminality.

Consequently, quality education is not real quality unless it is also equitable. Gonski 1 recommended needs-based funding to reduce the achievement gap. The recommendations of Gonski 1 faced a great deal of argy-bargy between the states and the Commonwealth and faced further disruption because of the change of federal government in 2013. As economist Adam Rorris pointed out, "…seven years after the Gonski report was handed down, school-funding policy remains a grotesque policy disaster … Instead of getting closer to its goal of more funding for disadvantaged schools, Australia has moved further away."[34]

As the research has shown, the inequality in outcomes in Australian schooling is significant and is growing, strongly related to socio-economic status. Gonski 1 saw it as a funding issue. Funding is just one dimension of the problem. There is a number of causes of inequality and a number of ways of tackling it. Some of these will be unique to particular contexts, such as those needed to tackle geographic isolation or the prevalence of migrant families. Many of these aspects of inequality result from the practice of automatic progression – of forcing all students through their school years at the same rate. In this context, disadvantaged students don't 'fall behind'. They are behind to start with and lock-step progression means they fall further behind. It is not extra money they need; it is extra time. Given extra time in the early school years, many of these students would achieve well. Stage-based learning is one way of providing this extra time.

However, there is also a dysfunctional aspect of school financing that creates regional inequality. This involves the inequity brought about because of the staffing formulae commonly used in Australian government school systems. Because some schools are less desirable than others, they are often staffed by teachers who are mainly in their early years of teaching. The staffing formula used determines the number of teachers appointed to a school rather than the salary costs available to the school.

I do not wish to imply that beginning teachers are necessarily less competent than experienced teachers. (Indeed, in my case, I think the first decade of my own teaching was the most productive and inspiring, for me and my students). The potential inequity comes about because the money spent on salaries in these 'less desirable' schools may be far less than that spent in equally-sized desirable schools.

For example, Elizabeth West was a 'disadvantaged school' when I moved there in 1984. From memory, it received $32,000 a year in extra funding from the Disadvantaged Schools Program as a result. However, because of the patterns of teacher employment, I estimated at the time that a school in a highly sought-after area in Adelaide with a similar enrolment to Elizabeth West would have about $200,000 more spent on it per year in teacher salaries.

The situation still exists. I have used 2020 South Australian salary scales in this example. Consider two schools, each with 600 students, and each with 25 teachers in non-promotion positions. School A is in a desirable area where most teachers are in their 6th, 7th or 8th year of teaching (average salary $93,500). School B is in an area less attractive for teachers and consequently most are in their 2nd, 3rd or 4th year of teaching (average salary $78,700).

School A's salary bill = 25 x $93,500 = $2,337,500.
School B's salary bill = 25 x $78,700 = $1,967,500

The difference between these two totals
$2,337,500 − $1,967,500 = $370,000

is enough to employ four or five extra teachers. In terms of expenditure per student, disadvantaged schools are subsidising advantaged schools!

There are two possible initiatives that could improve the situation. The first is to create incentives encouraging teachers to work in these less advantaged or remote schools.

Another approach would be to test the above hypothesis by calculating the salary dollars per student across a region with a wide range of socio-economic and remote schools. If the inequity is found to be real, the next step would be to explore alternative staffing patterns based on the real expenditure rather than on the number of teachers. In this way, schools that attract mainly less experienced teachers would be able to employ more of them. These schools could then have more support teachers and/or smaller classes. Application of this alternative approach would need to be monitored over several years, taking into account student learning outcomes, rates of sick leave, rates of resignation and the like. The initiative might have an impact, not just on student achievement in less desirable schools, but also on the overall patterns of teacher retention and recruitment.

The second Gonski Report,[35] written in 2018, focused on curriculum. Drawing attention to the decline in Australia's academic performance relative to other OECD countries, it noted that Australian school students are not improving at the same rate as other countries.

"… Australia still has an industrial model of school education that reflects a 20th century aspiration to deliver mass education to all children. This model is focused on trying to ensure that millions of students attain specified learning outcomes for their grade and age before moving them in lock-step to the next year of schooling."

The Report decries the fact that such a system is not designed to differentiate between students and that schools have inadequate incentives to improve the situation. Rather, the current work practices, the assessment models and the school structures inhibit innovation. The Review makes a recommendation to focus on student growth in learning, rather than on the common achievement (or not) of year-based standards. It states that schools should "Deliver at least one year's growth in learning for every student every year."

While I agree wholeheartedly with the focus on growth, I have two massive problems with this statement. First, the word 'deliver' reinforces the very concept that the review is attempting to challenge. The image is of a curriculum, designed and constructed at a central place and 'delivered' through state systems, schools and finally teachers to students in classrooms. Such imagery is at odds with students being key agents in the learning process. It is at odds with teachers as active professionals in deciding what, when, how and where particular challenges and opportunities will be sensitively introduced to students. It is at odds with the possibility that important new knowledge and new understandings might be created by groups of teachers and students. It is also at odds with the ability of teachers and students to respond effectively to local happenings and to the immediacy of national or international events. The writers' intentions are not accurately represented by the word 'deliver'.

My second problem with the statement is the concept of "at least one year's growth for every student every year". People learn at different rates. Indeed, if we take the student population as a whole, the rate at which any particular skill or concept is learned will be distributed as on a normal curve. So what is the standard measure of a year's growth? The average student? The slowest student? The statement makes no sense to me – and I've been in the business for sixty years. I fear the writers of the report became entangled in the very logic they were trying to escape. Indeed, in a later paragraph, they make an apparently contradictory statement. "To achieve this shift to growth, the Review Panel believes it is essential to move from a year-based curriculum to a curriculum expressed as learning progressions *independent of year or age.*"

There are two other issues that are problematic about the way this priority is elaborated. The report refers to collaborative planning, teaching and assessment so that student learning can be personalised. What about teaching being personalised? The danger is that collaboration between teachers or within teaching teams can be interpreted as implying that all should agree to do the same thing. I have no problem with collaborative planning if it focuses on taking advantage of and nurturing the unique skills, talents and preferred practices of individual teachers. The best teachers I have known all had their own particular, sometimes eccentric, ways of engaging students in learning. The wider the range of skills and experience in a teaching team, the greater its potential – as long as the differences are allowed to flourish. As one Tasmanian primary teacher explained to me, "If teachers are left to their own devices, they will naturally support each other and collaborate informally. As soon as they are forced to collaborate, under supervision, they no longer have ownership, control and investment in the process."

Another issue involves the panel's belief that teachers should be given "…an online, formative assessment tool to help diagnose a student's current level of knowledge, skill and understanding, to identify the next steps in learning, to achieve the next stage in growth, and to track student progress over time against a typical development trajectory." Again, the wording of this suggestion is contrary to the notion of avoiding 'mass production.' Diagnosing students against a 'typical development trajectory' and adjusting their learning plans accordingly amounts to pouring them through the same funnel, albeit at different rates.

I have nine grandchildren, described in the next chapter. Stimulated to learn in an untrammelled way, there is no way these differently talented children follow a common trajectory. The idea of tailoring student learning to a common trajectory risks an uncritical pruning of the unique skills, talents and quirky ideas they have. It focuses on correcting or ignoring deviation instead of nurturing it. The next chapter is one that many parents, grandparents and teachers will identify with. It highlights the fact that any assessment tool such as that suggested should be limited to the very basic elements of literacy and numeracy.

Chapter 16
Kids Are Different

I have nine grandchildren. I share their stories to demonstrate how different they are, despite growing up in similar environments. Is there a 'typical trajectory' for their learning, or a common curriculum to suit them all?

David's son Declan is the oldest. He is an only child, aged 16 in 2021. Midway through primary school, he became an expert in computing. Since then, much of his learning has been done online. He enjoys the socialisation that comes with online gaming. In year 10 at the local high school, he is tall and popular with his classmates. During the recent Covid-19 shutdown, Declan realised that home learning was perfect for him. He discovered he had excellent research skills. He also became a leader among his peers, helping them organise their learning, their interactions and their online gaming.

Daughter Sarah has three children. She attended state schools herself, has a PhD in law, and is passionate about government school education. Thomas, her oldest, is in second year at Wynyard High School in Tasmania. He has ADHD that is well controlled by medication. Despite some learning difficulties, he copes well socially and has some unique talents. He is athletic, a good swimmer, an excellent tennis player and a taekwondo black belt. I remember a situation when he was about eight years old and was visiting the aquatic centre in Burnie. Climbing the ladders to a high diving platform, he found six stocky teenagers blocking his path because they were hesitant, even scared, to enter the water from such a height. Thomas waited patiently and then finally excused himself, hurried through them, and took the plunge. I think he was unaware of the embarrassment they felt.

Several years ago, on a trip to north Queensland with his family, Thomas became fascinated with the didgeridoo. He brought one back to Tasmania and, through persistent practice, became expert as a performer. Aged ten, he began busking at the local fortnightly market, netting somewhere between twenty and fifty dollars each time. However, he wasn't interested in the monetary value of the coins. He started a coin collection, aspiring to collect coins of every date since decimalisation. Thomas enjoys adult company and will either make a very loyal employee or will find a self-employed business niche.

Sarah's younger children, James and Jessica, are twins, aged twelve in 2021. James does fairly well in grade 6 at the local primary school, without being greatly motivated. He finds the work easy, but this doesn't worry him. When he was nine years old and in grade 3, he 'had a go' on an alto saxophone. James took to it straight away. He wanted to join the school band, but he was frustrated because he had to be in grades 5 or 6 to do this. His mum approached the organisers of Wynyard's municipal band and asked if they had a place for a nine-year-old. Despite the fact that the next youngest player was about thirty-five, James was welcomed into the 'beginners' band' and music lessons were arranged for him. Before long, he learnt to read music and became very adept as a saxophonist. He won 'player of the year' in the beginners' band in 2018 and also in the intermediate band in 2019. In 2021, he is in the senior municipal band, aged twelve. In the meantime, he has developed a love of the guitar and has become an extremely good bass guitar player. I have spoken with his guitar teacher who says that his rate of learning is phenomenal.

Jessica went to the same local primary school as James. In 2019, she was in a 'composite' 4-5 class. While she was formally in year 4, her educational achievements were on a par or better than most of her year 5 friends. In 2020, the school organised a 'straight' grade 5.

This upset Jess because her friends and her educational peers were in grade 6. The grade 5 work was too easy for her and she became depressed and disengaged, so much so that the school contacted the parents advising them of their concern for Jessica's mental health.

Her parents asked if she could go into grade 6. The response was that the policy framework would only allow this if she were in the top two percent of students according to IQ. She was tested and found to be on the 97th percentile – just too low to go 'up' a year. Consequently, she chose to become a boarding student at Scotch-Oakburn College, 170 kilometres away in Launceston. That school placed her in year 6, where she was happy and did very well, especially in science. But the price was high – a separation from family at the age of eleven.

Daughter Ariane has three boys. As a family, they do a lot of camping and walking in the Tasmanian bush. Toby is thirteen, and a good soccer player. He attended a state primary school but has now enrolled at a Catholic secondary school and is on the Student Representative Council of the school. He is not a good speller but his skills with his laptop overcome that easily. Toby has three passions.

His first passion is biology. Since he was three years of age, he has watched documentaries such as those produced by David Attenborough. His interest in plants and animals, his understanding of their adaptions and his memory for facts amaze me. For example, when he was eleven, we went snorkelling on the Whitsundays with Toby and his brothers. They became very friendly with a sea turtle, stroking it and feeding it with prawn shells. As part of the conversation, I commented that he (the turtle) was a friendly chap.

"Oh, Pop, it's a girl," said Toby.

"How do you know Toby?"

"Look at her tail. It's too short to be a male."

I have yet to see a Tasmanian bird that Toby can't identify.

Toby's second passion is drawing and painting. His Instagram heading is as follows:

"I love art, science, nature and all animals living and extinct. I would like to share my art and photography with you so that you can enjoy it too!"

As his interest in animals developed, he drew many pencil sketches of the animals he loved. More recently, he has explored painting; the Waratah is a painting he gave to his mum for Mothers' Day last year.

The ant drawing leads into his third great passion. About three years ago, Toby became fascinated with ants. The one he has sketched here is *Campanotis consabrinis.* Following hours of lifting rocks in forests, he has a live collection (in test tubes in his bedroom drawer) of eleven species of ants. Most of them are queens. He knows the names of them all as well as their habitats, adaptions and colonial patterns. He still has five Tasmanian species yet to find and collect. Via YouTube, he shares information with entomologists in other countries. I am confident that there is only a handful of Australians who know as much about ants as Toby. I asked Toby what his friends at school thought of his nerdish love of ants.

"They don't know," he answered with a twinkle in his eye.

Lachie is Ariane's second child. In 2018, when Lachie was in Grade 3, he became frustrated at school because the classroom routines did not suit his learning style. I offered to home school him for six months. His mum and dad agreed. Basically, he was about two years ahead of schedule. I know this because I downloaded the year 5 NAPLAN tests and let him have a go at them (without telling him what they were). He tackled them confidently and well. We had lots of great times together. I think he learnt quite a bit. I did too. One day, during morning break, Lachie started a conversation.

"Everything's got a name doesn't it Pop."

"Not really Lachie."

"Well you tell me something that doesn't have a name."

We were next to a window looking out over a lawn.

"That blade of grass down there."

Lachie breathed in deeply.

"Pop, you just called it a blade of grass so that means its name is a blade of grass."

I realised I was getting into deep water.

"OK Lachie, tell me what this is all about."

"I think I have worked out why you can't remember things when you were a baby."

"Go on."

"Maybe it is because babies don't yet have words to put in their memory. If you don't know the grass is green, how can you remember the green grass?"

I said nothing.

"Do you think I might be right Pop?"

"I honestly don't know Lachie. Maybe someday, you will be able to find out for sure."

I shook my head and cleared the morning tea dishes.

Lachie is a talented long-distance runner. He plays soccer and Australian Rules football.

He shares Toby's interest in nature and is particularly concerned about climate change. He plays the piano well, and last year composed a piano piece titled, 'Fishing in the wind' dedicated to me on my eightieth birthday. Lachie has some quirky skills. Since he was in grade 3, no one, including me and other adults, has been able to beat him twice in a row at chess.

Matty is the youngest of the three brothers, two years younger than Lachie. He is a ray of sunshine most of the time. Right from the time he could talk, he noticed patterns and commented on them. The patterns were in the things he saw, the sounds he heard and the things he touched.

"The white rocks are lighter than the grey rocks."

"We just passed three red cars and then three white cars."

"Every fish we've caught is bigger than the last one."

His love of patterns meant that he also loves the rhythms of music and dance and spelling.

As soon as he started school, numeracy was his strength. He is very quick with number facts and mental arithmetic. I remember introducing him to negative numbers when he first started in Prep. It didn't take long.

"Matty, what happens if you take eight things away from five?"

"You can't take eight things away from five."

"Let's say you could."

"If you could, you'd be down three."

"Good one Matty. We often call that minus three."

Matty nodded and his eyes half closed as he took it in.

"OK, what would I get if I took twelve away from seven?"

"Minus five, of course."

It was as quick as that.

Leigh is my second son. He has two children, Henry who is five and Emma who is three.

They grew up on a rural property west of Queensland's Charters Towers where Leigh was building fences and sheds. From the time he could crawl, Henry was fascinated with hammers and saws and pliers and machines. He is a serious helper and handyman, changing tyres, doing anything mechanical, following his father around fishing and fixing. He loves to talk and is very articulate.

Emma has a twinkle in her eye that spells adventure. She is now extremely active, loving to run, jump, dance and climb. She is full of personality and delights in the world. When she was 12 months old, she took control of her pre-school curriculum. She loved to point to things and say w'dat?

"W'dat?"

"That's a tree."

"W'dat?"

"That's a car."

"W'dat?"

"That's the mountain".

And then a week or two later, we could switch the question and she could point to the tree or the car or the mountain. She loved playing these learning games, and still does.

How could a common curriculum, 'delivered' at a common rate, possibly serve the needs of these nine children?

Chapter 17
Uncluttering The Curriculum

The Gonski 2 Review and the recent New South Wales curriculum review have much in common. Gonski 2's second priority addresses the need for students to be "creative, connected and engaged learners" while the NSW Review is titled "Nurturing Wonder and Passion".[36] Both reviews are critical of the fact that students are subjected to a 'lock-step curriculum' that forces all students to progress through the same content at the same rate.

Reflecting many public consultations and written submissions, the NSW Review calls for a more flexible curriculum. It draws attention to the unfortunate consequences of streaming that perpetuate social groupings based on achievement, and by implication, on socio-economic status. The Review explains how 'mixed ability' classes have been used to prevent these consequences. It goes on to describe the situation teachers face when they try, in these mixed ability classes, to 'differentiate' the learning program to meet the needs of individual students. Not only has the mandated curriculum become cluttered and overcrowded. Teachers have also had to cope with the wide range of learning needs in each class. Students' reading ages typically vary by five or six years in each age cohort.

The Review suggests that a pre-constructed scope and sequence specifying what will be taught, when it will be taught and for how long it will be taught is not a good idea. (Ironically, this reflects almost verbatim the words of people like Garth Boomer, John Holt, Neil Postman, Ivan Illich, Paulo Freire and Malcolm Skilbeck written four decades earlier). The recommendation is that teachers should identify the progress of individual students and record it so that decisions can be made about their next steps in learning. The demands on teachers to undertake this kind of differentiation is daunting.

A teacher with 25 students in her class theoretically has to keep track of progress in eight learning areas for each individual. This means two hundred separate pieces of data she has to record and use in her planning and teaching. Of course, this does not happen. She has to prioritise. Consequently, the 'coverage' in some subjects becomes token only. As far back as 1995, research by the Coalition of Essential Schools in the USA found that the more crowded a curriculum becomes, the more superficial and shallow is the learning, with disastrous effects on the learners, particularly for those most at risk.[37]

The NSW Review uses the expression 'uncluttering' to describe an urgent need to simplify an overloaded curriculum. However, to see uncluttering merely as reducing the subject content ignores other vital issues that have emerged since the Australian Curriculum was introduced. Ironically, increasing the formal curriculum content resulted in more time and effort needed to demonstrate adherence to it. For many, increased 'paperwork', 'tick the box' assessment and time spent in meetings eroded real teaching time. Teachers therefore had to teach more content with less time available. Consequently, 'uncluttering' means creating more time to teach, as well as less content to teach. This involves changes in management, not just content.

There is also a problematic issue arising from the recent reviews that needs to be addressed. Is the distinction between 'creativity' and the 'basics' a true dichotomy? There is a danger that, in uncluttering the curriculum, the elements considered dispensable will be the creative subjects that are sometimes seen to be less important than the basics of literacy and numeracy. This is clearly not the intention of those who wrote Gonski 2 and the NSW Reviews, titled respectively "Creative, Connected and Engaged Learners" and "Nurturing Wonder and Passion".

Most kids are creative, connected and engaged before they go to school. Child care centres are characterised by toddlers going every which way physically, socially and mentally. The task of the primary and secondary schools is to provide them with the tools to pursue their engagements, not to disengage them and try to redirect their interests into a mainstream commonality. Helping students reach their potential is not about having them climb a common scale to see how high they can get. Rather, it is about nurturing their unique talents and aspirations. For most, developing those talents and following those aspirations will require increasing levels of literacy, numeracy and knowledge of the world. They will understand that. Basics should not be seen as a prerequisite for creativity. Creativity is often the stimulus to master the basics. (I want to tell you. I need to measure. How do I write this? Can you help me read this plan? How do I find out?) Students inevitably seek the basics to follow their passions.

If top-down mass delivery is the problem, top-down uncluttering is hardly likely to be the answer. Teachers and schools know best how to 'unclutter' their curriculum. Uncluttering involves pruning content. It also involves making links so that the learning is deep. It's about uncluttering processes as well as content. The potential to unclutter is very much a local issue. Schools with teachers strong in, say, science and history, might choose to swap classes each semester and just focus on their particular area for that semester. Other schools might be in a position to focus on particular key learning areas every second year of students' programs. Others might delay the introduction of formal science lessons until the third or fourth year of schooling. Others might move to a stage-based continuous classroom structure. Yet others might use an 'essential learnings' approach.

One obvious change schools might make is to provide adequate time for individual teachers to plan. Some primary schools have a team of senior staff members who do not teach, or who teach very rarely. To justify their leadership role, they use some of the 'preparation and correction' time to organise meetings with teaching teams. In my experience, these meetings often model a top-down approach that does not honour the unique skills of individual teachers and does not honour their need for professional time alone.

The recommendation in the NSW Review to unclutter the curriculum will help NSW teachers and their students. Hopefully, similar actions might be taken in other jurisdictions. However, changes such as these, albeit helpful quantitatively, do not address the major issue. This is because the initiative is still top-down. It does not solve the cultural accountability issue.

Chapter 18
Buffered Spaces

We need good teachers. However, unless there are fundamental changes in the work practices and the culture of teaching, the numbers of creative, passionate and intelligent people choosing teaching will continue to decline in Australia. Revitalising the culture requires carefully crafted strategies. Because increased teacher autonomy and creativity are essential, top-down initiatives are problematic. They need to be enabling and supportive rather than directive.

Teaching and administrative cultures will only improve when educators enjoy far greater autonomy in their work. They also need to be confident that their work is making a difference, that inequality is being tackled and that students are engaged in relevant and contemporary learning programs tailored to their needs. Wonder, passion and connectedness are not stimulated when learning programs are driven by assessment. 'Wonder and passion' have to be inherent in the learning, not in the 'result'. Assessment should never be seen as a tool of teacher accountability but rather as a helpful element of good teaching and effective learning.

The need for 'bottom-up' change is recognised by the Gonski 2 writers:

"School systems and schools must maintain a focus on innovation and improvement." They propose a National Research Institute to collect and share data about local initiatives: "National level data plays a key role in top-down monitoring, benchmarking and accountability processes, but alone are insufficient to achieve improved outcomes. They need to be complemented by a bottom-up approach."

In order for there to be local initiatives, two preliminary issues need to be addressed.

The first involves the changed culture of school teaching. Over the past decade, teachers' attitudes have changed. The blanketing effect of NAPLAN, the Australian Curriculum and the associated implication of upwards accountability have discouraged many teachers and administrators from experimenting with their pedagogy and their curriculum plans. Teachers are uncertain about what they can and can't do. They need to see themselves as curriculum co-developers and not just conduits delivering a mass curriculum. Catalysts are needed to kickstart a more proactive approach to teaching. This is a tricky dilemma. How can a central agency remove its domination of content, process and initiative? ("Now they're telling us we have to be proactive.")

The second issue is the widespread pattern of teacher mobility, particularly in government school systems. This pattern of teacher and principal transfer is based on individual career paths in a process that is typically disinterested in any emerging and innovative differences between schools or school clusters. The result is that, in a relatively short time, any unique structures or practices that have crystallised in particular schools will likely be dissolved by the random 'Brownian' movement of staff. In this way, the old hegemony reasserts itself. Some of the 'vertical' secondary schools that were formed as a result of the 1980s McGowan (NSW) and Beazley (WA) Reports suffered just such a fate, as did many of the Queensland stage-based schools of the 1980s and 1990s.

This results in an ongoing grey school landscape with occasional bursts of colour.

The challenge is to protect the initiatives already happening, and then to share the information they provide so that further initiatives are sparked and encouraged. This can best be achieved by creating 'buffered spaces', organisational niches where professional educators have room to innovate without the threat of their initiatives being dissolved back into commonality.

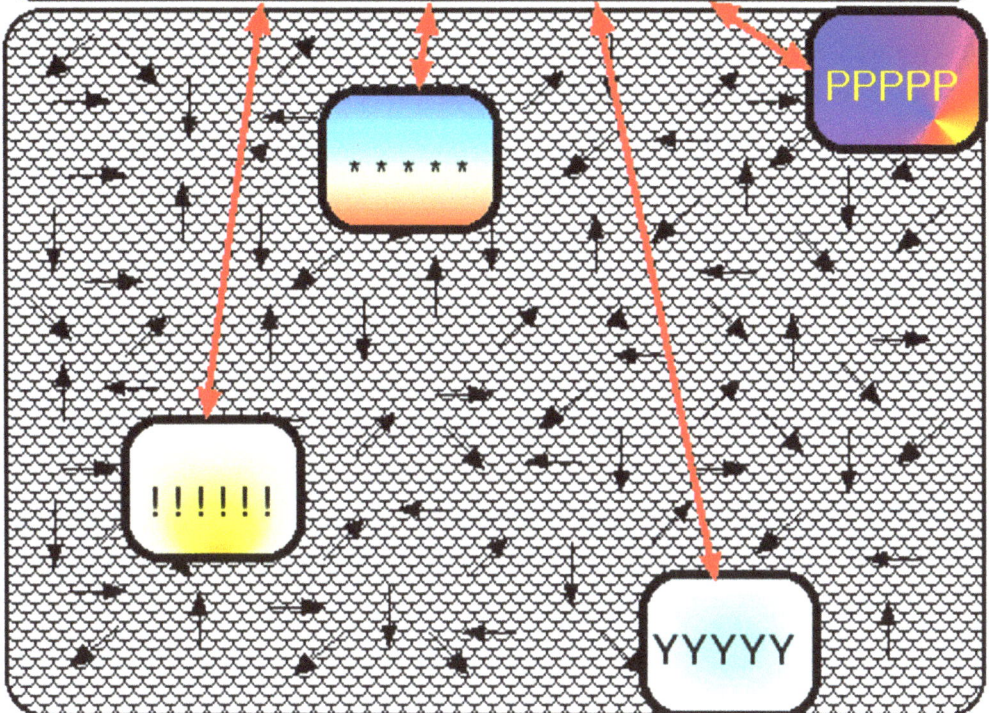

There is a need to develop an apolitical process of renewal that is understood both from a national perspective and at the level of the local school community. Regional activity is needed to manage the interaction between the national and local contexts. Gonski 2 recommends a National Institute. My belief is that a National Institute needs more than a research and monitoring role. It needs to have a catalytic role. It must have a regional presence because, without it, there is no way to spark, acknowledge, protect and communicate initiatives. Such a strategy need not be complex or expensive.

There are already many valuable initiatives taking place in Australia. Teams of educators in school communities are exploring effective and different methods of learning and teaching. Approaches used by Steiner schools, Montessori schools and the International Baccalaureate have long provided alternative approaches. Newer groups such as those involving 'Big Picture', 'Active Learning', 'Competency-based Education' and the 'Contemporary Learning' being undertaken in Lutheran schools have much to offer. Big Picture has already established a number of schools and has had an alternative tertiary entrance qualification approved. It is important to develop ways of protecting these initiatives and sharing their important experiences throughout the profession so that further explorations are stimulated and improvements bedded down. Currently, there is no formal infrastructure to do this.

My suggestion is that the ACER be funded to create a national network that can stimulate and monitor school and community-based initiatives. (My estimate is that the basic cost would be about $500,000 per year).

It could do this by creating regional committees, each representing local populations. Perhaps one each for Tasmania, Western Australia, South Australia, Australian Capital Territory, the Northern Territory as well as regional committees in Victoria, New South Wales and Queensland – maybe twelve committees altogether. (ACER already has a formal presence in five capital cities and has a widespread membership covering all education sectors and is therefore capable of providing suitable initial convenors.)

The task might be tackled as follows.

- Each committee should be representative of practitioners in State education, Catholic education, Independent schools, Teacher Education faculties, Teachers' Unions, parent organisations and relevant invited groups – about twelve people on each committee.
- The initial convenors of each committee should first meet together nationally to clarify the roles and protocols of the committees.
- Once convened, the committees should elect a chairperson,
- The committees should meet about monthly to:
  » provide (by brainstorming, research and networking) an open-ended range of initiatives that schools or school clusters or regions or parishes might take (using online communication).

» receive reports from individual schools (school clusters, regions, parishes) about initiatives already being undertaken, reported initially by the relevant committee member. In time, people managing particular initiatives could be invited to the meetings to describe their project, answer questions, and clarify any support needed.

The important aim here is not to try to identify a 'one-best-way', but to share good practice across the educational community so that continuing improvement can occur. There is no 'one-best-way' that could apply across all contexts. If 'one-best-way' was defined and mandated, we would be back where we started with a top-down hegemony.

» liaise with the relevant systems (State, Catholic or Independent) so that initiatives are appropriately supported in terms of resourcing, the appointment of new staff and public communication. This should not involve significantly greater costs. The special support should be qualitative rather than quantitative.

» communicate the initiatives to other committees within the nation so that a national database can be established and an online 'newsletter' created to share the successes and shortcomings of initiatives.

There are many areas where schools, clusters or parishes might take significant initiatives that feed into the national discussion.

These might include ways of uncluttering the curriculum including:

◊ using the experience of 'big picture' schools to develop new approaches

◊ adopting Steiner approaches where teachers follow students through several years

◊ delaying the formal introduction of some key learning areas such as science or geography

◊ using a 'warp and weft' approach to highlight the links across subject areas

- customising local curricular patterns by utilising the special skills of some teachers to focus on particular stages or year groups within a cluster of schools.

They might include a new look at assessment and reporting by:

- working with parents on what they need to know about their child's learning
- asking students to evaluate their own learning programs
- breaking away from 'normed' approaches and describing instead what students have learnt.

They might include ways of supporting teachers by:

- introducing induction programs that foster innovative approaches to teaching and learning
- fostering teamwork that encourages teachers to learn from each other
- creating career pathways that encourage outstanding teachers to stay teaching.

It is important in all these considerations to involve the teacher unions. There is a need to acknowledge that differences between schools create opportunities for enhancing teachers' workloads, cultures and career paths, as well as raising the status of the profession generally.

It is also vital that Faculties of Education at universities take on a proactive role. They should be able to work with schools to initiate exciting programs for teachers and students.

Much has already been written about alternatives to a strictly subject-based curriculum and its effects on pedagogy and assessment. These writings include historical documents involving the 'new Basics', the 'Essential Learnings' together with more recent work by groups such as 'Big Picture.' Too little has been written about alternatives to the age-grouping and lock-step progression that also have far reaching effects on curriculum, pedagogy and assessment, particularly in primary schools.

I'm therefore taking the opportunity to describe an alternative approach that was developing in many schools prior to the blanketing effect of NAPLAN and the year-based Australian Curriculum.

Chapter 19

POSTSCRIPT: Breaking the Lock-Step

I find it significant that Gonski 2 and the more recent NSW Review both recommend a curriculum that breaks the lock-step, age-based learning *progression* of students yet continues to accept, without question, the age-based *grouping* of students. This beggars belief given that the alternatives are so simple.

Acknowledging that students learn at different rates, Gonski 2 and the NSW Review are against fixed common time blocks for student learning. But if all students have seven years of primary schooling, that is a major 'block'. It is obvious that, on graduation, there will be a normal distribution of the levels of achievement reached as a result of their seven years. This will not be disastrous for many students in the middle range. However, a minority, particularly those who were among the oldest on entry, may not need the full seven years and could well graduate after six years. (They might be only a month younger than some of the students graduating in the same year). Others, particularly those who were youngest on entry, may benefit from an extra year. (They might be only a month older than fellow students graduating in the same year). In typical classrooms around the country, these exceptions involve no more than about twenty per cent of students. Yet they demand a much greater percentage of time and effort for teachers attempting true differentiation. The time pressure on teachers can easily preclude the real attention these students need.

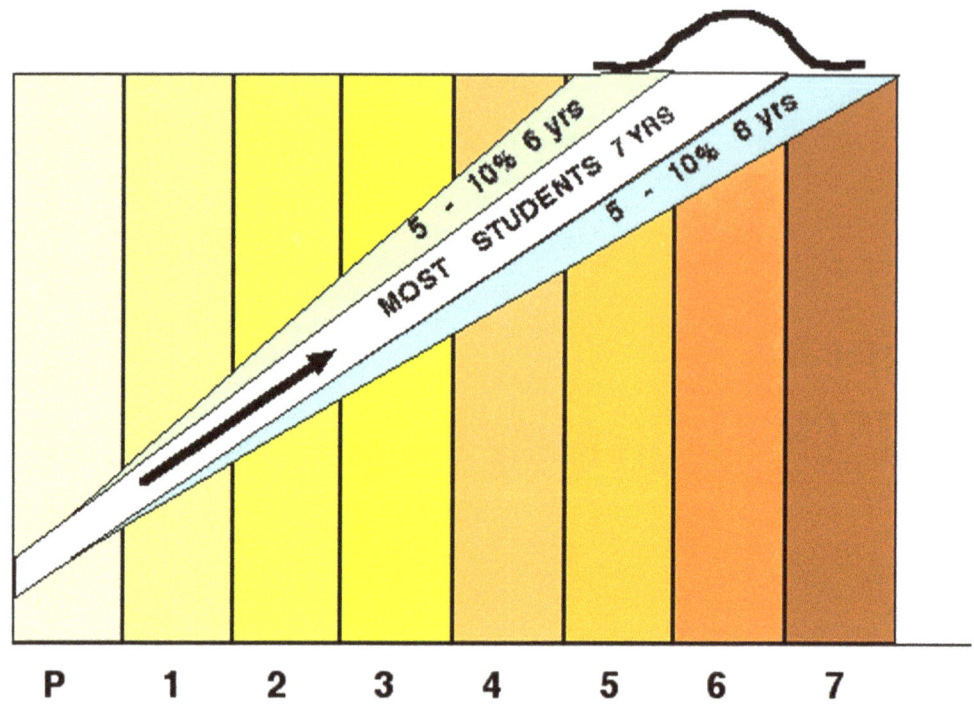

In lock-stepped grouping, the time requirements for these exceptions can only be achieved by 'repeating' a year or 'skipping' a year. Such strategies do not provide continuity in student learning. The first inevitably has students engaging (or not) in some learning activities they have already mastered. The second risks missing some essential steps in the learning progression. In any case, both strategies can have damaging social consequences.

Only a structure which routinely frees students from the shackle of age-based groupings can provide the appropriate timelines for students. Historically, this has been possible in small schools (like a couple of hundred Queensland schools currently). The practice of student promotion through schools has varied from state to state. However, since World War II, the increasing size of schools and the centralisation of administration have seen administrative convenience take precedence with the consequent unquestioned assumption of a lock-stepped and common seven-year primary schooling.

During the 1990s, there were many larger primary schools that were not lock-stepped. They used an overlapping stage-based pattern. Such a pattern is quite simple to achieve, once understood – certainly simpler

POSTSCRIPT: Breaking the Lock-Step

than the complex year-by-year pattern of composites many schools have dealt with. It's not rocket science. The following explanation may well be easier for a lay person to understand than a teacher or principal or educational administrator who has been conditioned into a year-based thinking mode.

The total enrolment of the school is divided by the number of classes desired. This indicates the class size that can apply throughout the school. Then we start with the students in their first primary school year and work our way up. The numbers will always provide potential for the overlap required. This is done at the beginning of each calendar year.

Let's consider a school with 258 students and eleven available teachers/rooms.

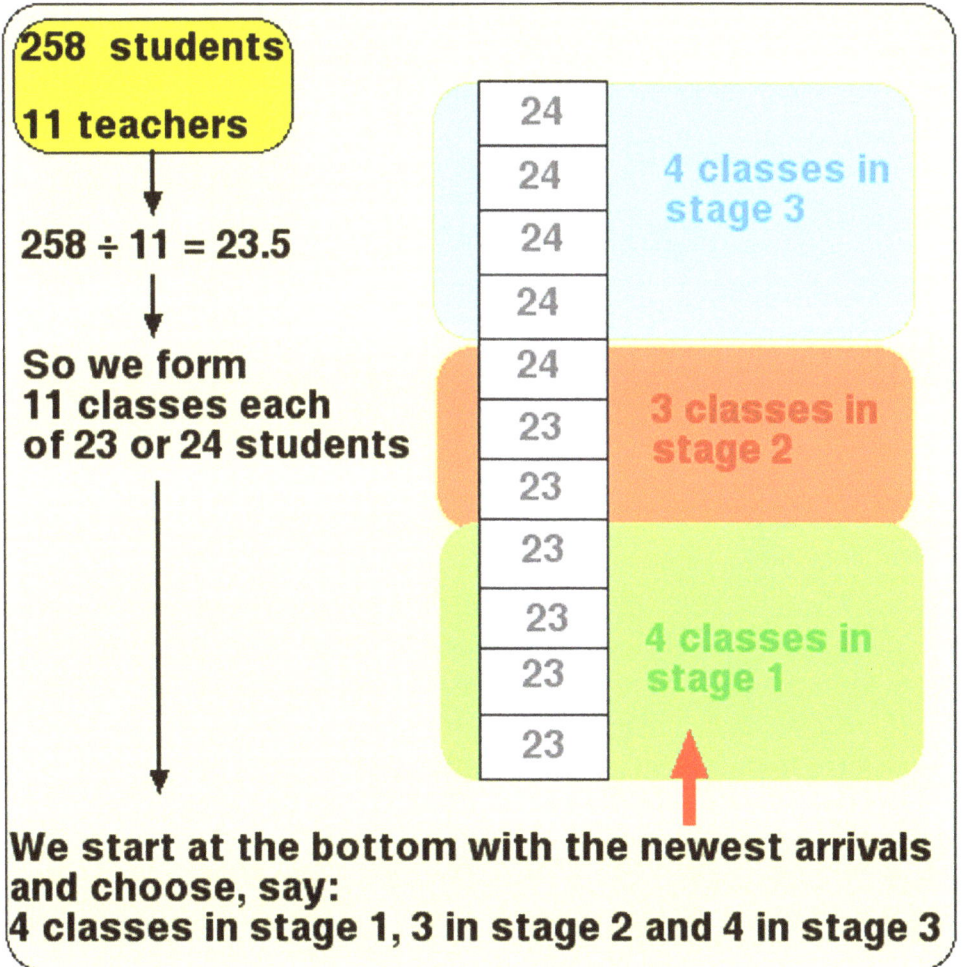

It is important to note that the 'labels' representing year groups no longer apply once the stage-based pattern is in place. (Indeed, I remember asking a girl in stage 2 at St Thomas' in Mareeba what year she was in. She looked puzzled and asked me what I meant. It was only when I asked how many years had she been at school that I was able to correct my 'dumb' question.)

Let's look at a detailed example. School X has 222 students and can form nine classes. Until now, it has used a pattern of composite classes that have varied from year to year. The distribution across the years since entry is shown in the top left of the diagram below.

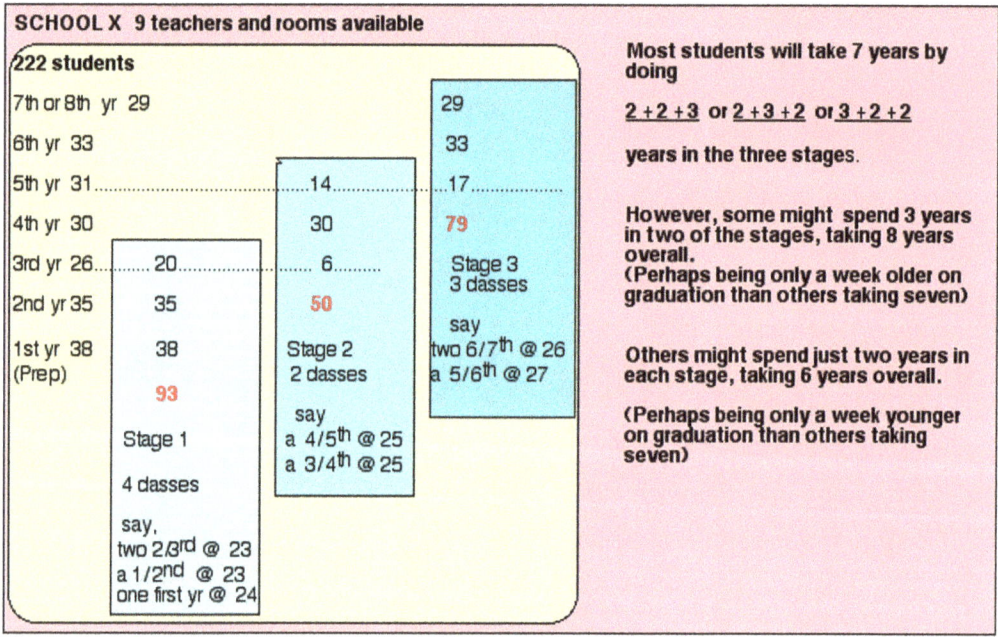

There is a number of ways of creating overlapping stages. We could form three classes at each stage. However, in this case, the numbers are weighted in the early years. So we might choose to have four classes in stage 1, two classes in stage 2 and three classes in stage 3. We form the classes at the beginning of each calendar year.

For Stage 1, we start at the intake year and create four classes, a first year (used to be called prep) of 24, a mixed first and second year class of 23 and two second/third year classes of 23

This leaves six third year students to flow into Stage 2.

Now, we do a similar thing in Stage 2. We create a 3rd/4th year class of 25 and a 4th/5th year class of 25.

This leaves seventeen students to flow into Stage 3 where we can create a 5th/6th year class of 27 and two 6th/7th year classes of 26.

For most students, it does not matter in which stage they spend three years. This provides flexibility for schools to decide, for example, the make-up of the six students in their third year who will progress into stage 2. Teachers may take into account issues like age, gender balance, friendship patterns and social maturity. Because these six students will likely spend three years in Stage 2 or stage 3, they are not 'ahead' of the twenty students who spent their three years in stage 1. (I often found parents, particularly of younger children, preferred the three years to be spent in Stage 1. This was especially true in low socio-economic settings.)

The internal organisation stage-based schools commonly used is outlined on pages 86 & 87.

(The author is willing to respond to emails about the possibilities in particular schools – mwmidd@gmail.com).

Conclusion

During the last half of the 1900s there were many inspirational people involved in school education, both in Australia and elsewhere. My fellow teachers and I read widely across a range of educational literature. We saw ourselves as members of an exciting and dynamic profession, modifying our ideas and practices as we gained new perspectives and insights. During that time, we felt valued by State and Federal Governments and by policy makers. As practising, school-based teachers, we had opportunities, often by invitation, to participate in national, state, and regional discussions about the future of school education in Australia.

While there are still some wonderfully creative and professional teachers in Australia, over the past two decades, there has been a change in the general culture of teaching that has discouraged people from entering the profession. It has also caused many to discontinue teaching, to teach part-time, or to persevere with a job they no longer enjoy.

The nature of the cultural shift was highlighted for me during a discussion I had recently with a long-time friend and colleague who had resigned in frustration from teaching. I asked her to read an early draft of this book and give me feedback.

"You are right." she said. "The National Curriculum narrowed things down so much."

At first, I was a bit puzzled thinking there was too much in the Australian curriculum. She went on to explain.

"Our lives as teachers, and what we had to teach were stuffed so full, there wasn't room to move anymore. Our professional choices as teachers virtually disappeared."

In my early years exploring the art of teaching, the Tasmanian curriculum was like a range of coloured paints. I chose how to use the colours, how to apply them, and in what order. The choice was based on a number of considerations, all of which related to the interests and talents of the students I was teaching. They were the canvas, if you like. If I got it wrong, the paint just wouldn't stick.

What I chose had to be of interest to them. It had to have meaning within the context of their lives, where they lived and what was happening at the time. I had many techniques available. Sometimes, I chose to teach very directly, explaining concepts and even using quite structured classroom 'drills' to reinforce the learning. At other times, it was best to raise questions and have the students use research or experiment to find possible answers. There were times when the learning was driven by their questions, rather than mine. Often, the classroom was the most appropriate place for learning. In some cases, learning was deeper and more memorable when it occurred in other settings. Wherever the place and whatever the context, questioning and critical thinking were central to the ongoing learning.

Towards the end of a term or semester, I reviewed my program to make sure that I hadn't overlooked any vital colours. I found it more important to assess myself and my program than to assess students' 'results'. If I gained the impression that students were motivated more by their 'grade' than by an interest in the subject, I knew I had to lift my game. Otherwise, they felt their learning could be 'forgotten' once the assessment had been recorded.

Recently, two related changes have impinged on this kind of approach. The first involved a shift in the implied purpose of schooling. The evolving titles of the Federal agencies managing education in Australia epitomise the change. The changes from "Schools Commission" to "National Board of Education, Employment and Training" to "Department of Education, Skills and Employment" carry a very strong message. Education is designed to serve the economy. The second change involves the centralisation of curriculum management. Because the national economy was seen to be the responsibility of the federal government, it followed that education ought also to be their responsibility. In the minds of some, a national curriculum was justified. This mechanistic view of a curriculum that could be packaged and delivered *en masse* to all Australian students severely limited teachers' opportunities to craft their teaching in response to local contexts.

Conclusion

I fear that many teachers feel they are just 'colouring in'. Their main reference is The Australian Curriculum. Their responsive creativity has been replaced by fixed criteria, rubrics and checklists. Teachers who entered the profession over the past decade have known nothing else. They see 'delivering' the curriculum and demonstrating they have done so as their job.

The real world of Australian young people varies significantly from place to place. Growing up in the western suburbs of Sydney is very different socially and environmentally from growing up in Alice Springs or Thursday Island or Cockle Creek in Southern Tasmania. The way young people use social media, the sports they play, the hobbies they adopt and the rhythms of their everyday life make up a rich tapestry of experience across the nation. The uniqueness of these settings are potentially the springboards for curriculum relevance.

However, with an elaborately detailed national curriculum, teachers are limited in their ability to customise their teaching to match the lived reality of their students. As a result, many school children now live in two worlds – their lived reality and their school reality.

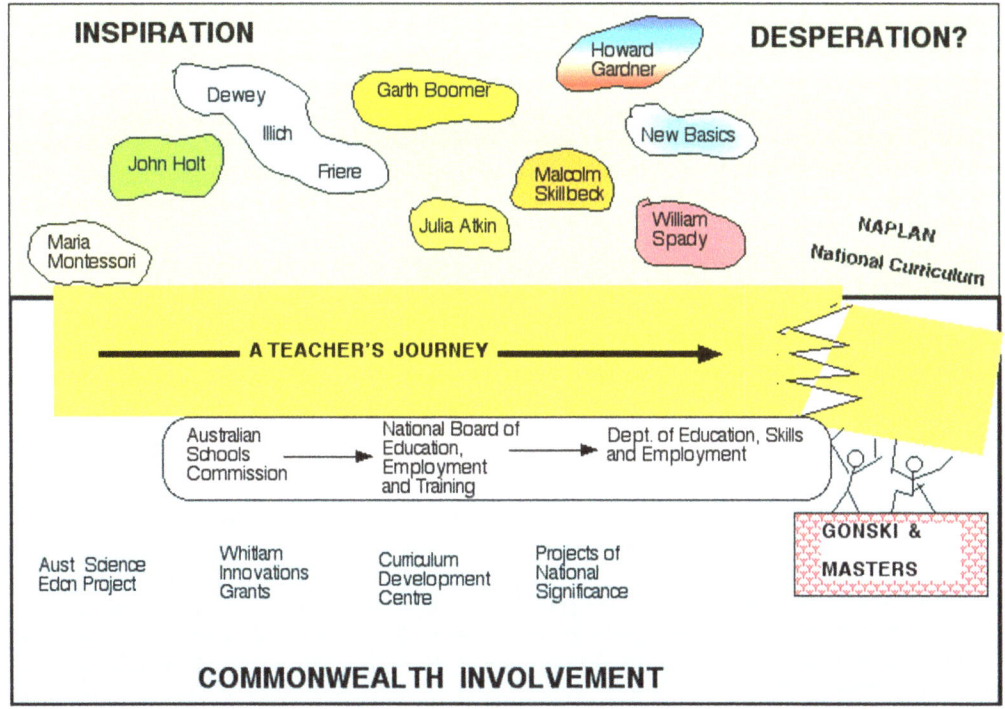

I am firmly convinced that there is no one-best-way in any field of teaching and learning, whether it be pedagogy, assessment or curriculum planning. Children are different, communities are different. The essence of teaching is finding the appropriate pattern that suits one's teaching style and that meets the needs, aspirations and talents of each student and each group of students. This happens best when diversity is encouraged and where networking within the profession provides new insights and new possibilities.

Bibliography

1. Blackburn, J. (Chairperson) (1985). Ministerial Review of Postcompulsory Schooling (Blackburn Report). Melbourne: Education Department, Melbourne.

2. Andrews, Daniel (2014) Labor Party Campaign Speech.

3. Wyndham, H.S. (1957) "Wyndham Report" Committee Appointed to Survey Secondary Education in New South Wales, 1957 (Chair: H. S. Wyndham)

4. Holt, John (1970) What Do I Do Monday? New York: Dutton.

5. Dewey, J. (1938) Experience and Education, New York: Macmillan

6. Neil Postman and Charles Weingartner, (1971) Teaching as a Subversive Activity, Great Britain: Penguin.

7. Ivan Illich, (1971), Deschooling Society, Harmondsworth: Penguin Books.

8. Freire, Paulo (1970), Pedagogy of the Oppressed, Harmondsworth: Penguin Books

9. Karmel Report (1973) Schools in Australia, Aust Gov Printing Service

10. Connell, William (1978), Tasmanian Education Next Decade Report (TEND), Tasmanian Education Department, 1978, p44.

11. Skilbeck, M. (1984) School Based Curriculum Development London: Harper and Rowe, p xii.

12. Boomer, G. (1982) Negotiating the Curriculum: A Teacher-Student Partnership (p 119-121) Sydney: Ashton Scholastic.

13. Boomer, G. (1982) Negotiating the Curriculum: A Teacher-Student Partnership (p 132) Sydney: Ashton Scholastic.

14. Middleton, M. (1982) Marking Time: Alternatives in Australian Schooling, Sydney: Methuen.

15. McGowan, B. (1981) Report of the Select Committee of the Legislative Assembly Upon the School Certificate, Sydney: NSW Government Printer, June.

16. Connell, William (1978), Tasmanian Education Next Decade Report (TEND), Tasmanian Education Department, 1978, p45.

17. These two quotes from Dwight Brown were uncovered during my research. After Dwight died, I asked his wife, whom I knew well, if I could access Dwight's filing cabinet. She was only too happy to oblige.

18. Jones, B., (1982) Sleepers Wake: Technology and the Future of Work, Sydney: Oxford University Press.

19. Middleton et al, 1986, Making the Future: The Role of Secondary Education in Australia, Canberra: Commonwealth Schools Commission.

20. Ford, J.E. (1990) Are There New Basics? Brisbane: Ministerial Consultative Council on Curriculum.

21. Beazley –chair (1984) Education in Western Australia: Report of the committee of Enquiry into Education in Western Australia: WA Education Department.

22. Middleton, M. (2000) Lutheran Schools at Millennium's Turn: A Snapshot, Adelaide: Lutheran Ed. Aust.

23. Gardner, Howard (1983) Frames of Mind, Harvard University.

24. Spady, W. (1993) Outcome-Based Education, Australian Curriculum Studies Association Workshop Report No 5.

25. Spady, W. (19??) It's Time to Take a Close Look at Outcome-based education, Eagle, CO: the high success network (mimeograph).

26. Middleton, M., (2007) Timetabling and Other Practical Ideas, Queensland Studies Association, May.

27. Nelson, Brendan (2005) Transcript of interview – Sunrise programme, 8 February

28. Bishop, Julie 2006 Address to the History Teachers' Association of Australia Conference, Fremantle, 6 October.

29. Curwin, Richard (2012, July) How to Beat 'Teacher Proof Programs', edutopia, George Lucas Educational Foundation.

30. Weldon, P.R. (2015 – March) The Teacher Workforce in Australia, ACER.

31. Weldon, P. & Ingvarson, L. (2016) School Staff Workload Study, Australian Education Union, ACER page 28.

32. McKinnon, Merryn (2016, January 11th) "The Conversation".

33. Gonski, D. (Chair) (2011) Review of Funding for Schooling, Australian Government Department of Education.

34. Rorris, Adam (June 2008) Rebuilding public schools 2020 - investment targets Australian Education Union.

35. Gonski, D. (Chair) (2018), Report of the Review to Achieve Educational Excellence, Australian Government Department of Education.

36. Masters, G. (Chair) (2019) NSW Curriculum Review, ACER

37. Cushman, Kathleen (1995, April) Less in More: The secret of being essential, Horace Volume 11 Issue 2, USA, The Coalition of Essential Schools.

38. Middleton, M and Hill, J. (1998) Changing Schools, Melbourne: Hawker Brownlow.

Acknowledgements

A number of people have assisted me in writing this book. My first acknowledgement must go to the wonderful students and colleagues with whom I shared my professional life.

In terms of the book itself a number of people have provided me with valuable feedback and ideas.

In Queensland, there were colleagues with whom I had long shared ideas. They included: Cate and Doug Patterson, Dr Bill Sultmann, Dr Roger Hunter and Meryl Holbeck together with my Cousin Leslie Kirmsse.

In NSW, Viv White, the co-founder of Big Picture Schools, a long-term inspiration and colleague, has been helpful and supportive.

In Tasmania, I have been pleased to confer with other long-term colleagues and friends including Roy and Kay Pallett, Anne Kittell and my daughter Dr Sarah Buist.

I must also include my grandchildren who (mostly) approve of what I wrote about them and who have taught me much about teaching and life generally.

www.ingramcontent.com/pod-product-compliance
Lightning Source LLC
Chambersburg PA
CBHW051247110526
44588CB00025B/2904